HYPNOHE

HYPNOHEALTH

How to Transform Your Life Through the Power of Hypnosis

ROBERT FARAGO

VERMILION
LONDON

First published 1993
Reissued 1995

First published in the United Kingdom in 1993 by Vermilion
an imprint of Ebury Press
Random House
20 Vauxhall Bridge Road
London SW1V 2SA

Random House Australia (Pty) Limited
20 Alfred Street, Milsons Point, Sydney
New South Wales 2061, Australia

Random House New Zealand Limited
18 Poland Road, Glenfield
Auckland 10, New Zealand

Random House South Africa (Pty) Limited
PO Box 337, Bergvlei, South Africa

Random House UK Limited Reg. No. 954009

A CIP catalogue record for this book
is available from the British Library

ISBN 0 09 177576 0

Typeset by Hope Services (Abingdon) Ltd
Printed and bound in Great Britain by
Mackays of Chatham Plc, Kent

Contents

**For information on Farago Clinic
tapes and hypnotherapy sessions,
please contact the Clinic on
(0171) 431 1959.**

DEDICATION

This book is dedicated to my father, who taught me to love words, and my mother, who taught me to recognise beauty.

THANKS

I wish to express my deepest thanks to my wife Caroline for her love, support and patience. Without her this book would not have been possible. Also, thanks to hypnotherapist Joseph Cymrank for his humour and inspiration. Finally, thanks to the people who teach me everything I know: my clients.

Part One

HOW YOU THINK IS HOW YOU ARE

'They can because they think they can.'

Virgil

1
Health – The Mind-Body Connection

One summer morning, my wife and I headed back to the UK after visiting my childhood home by the coast. We gave my parents a hug, threw our cases into the van and left for the airport. A young woman who I'll call Linda sat in the front seat, enjoying the beauty of a seafront sunrise. After shaking off the early-morning cobwebs, we introduced ourselves. When Linda learned I was a hypnotherapist, and that my wife was an aromatherapist, we began to discuss alternative health. She told us an interesting story.

Linda's first child was not a healthy baby. After a couple of weeks, the baby developed a life-threatening case of pleurisy – fluid on the lungs. He was hospitalised and treated with conventional antibiotics. When his condition rapidly grew worse, Linda turned to a homoeopathic doctor for advice. He recommended an old home remedy: lemon juice. For centuries, people have used lemon juice to cut through phlegm and kill bacteria (one reason we squeeze it on fish). The homoeopathic doctor told Linda to add lemon juice to her son's IV drip (the liquids flowing into the child's arm). Linda's hospital doctor refused to consider the treatment.

Desperate, Linda asked to remove her son from the hospital. The baby's condition was so serious the doctor refused to release him. So Linda secretly added a small amount of lemon juice to the baby's IV drip. Within hours, he began to recover. Within days, he was strong and healthy. Within a week, he was well enough to go home. When Linda told the hospital doctor how she had saved her child's life, he dismissed her simple remedy and threatened to report her to the authorities. With her baby safe, Linda couldn't have cared less. Even so, she felt badly that other mothers could lose their babies simply because they never questioned their doctor's treatment.

Linda's story is not meant to be a criticism of doctors or traditional, Western medicine. Antibiotics have saved millions of lives. I'm sure her hospital doctor did what he thought best for the baby's health and safety, even when it was clear he was fighting a losing battle. Fortunately, more and more doctors are willing to recommend alternative therapies – from herbal treatments to massage. Linda's experience is not an example of failure; it's one of opportunity. Linda learned that it's no good trusting your health or the health of your children to anyone else. You have to take control.

We are raised to believe that 'doctor knows best'. Nothing could be more misleading. What doctor knows best is medicine, not you. When a new client comes to The Farago Clinic, I take a complete medical history covering every area of health: operations, medications, previous treatments and more. The case history also includes diet, alcohol, exercise, work, hobbies, family, love life, sex life, worries, emotional factors, childhood and anything else that may come up. The initial consultation usually takes an hour. When I've finished the case history, I am fully aware of how much more there is to know about the client. How could I know anything truly significant about a person after having spent one hour in their company? And yet . . .

I deal with dozens of clients every year who are on heavy medication. Some of these people are taking large doses of anti-depressants. I ask these drug-taking clients how the drug is supposed to work. They don't know. I ask them how long they are supposed to take it, or how they'll know when they're 'cured'. They don't know. How long did you meet with the doctor before he prescribed the drug? Ten to fifteen minutes. Did he ask you about the mental, emotional or spiritual challenges you face? Not really. Has the drug worked? I don't know. So why are you taking it? Doctor knows best.

So many people are willing to surrender control of their lives to people they've just met. They're convinced that it's better to trust the expert's ignorance than their own.

But no one knows you better than you know yourself. What do you love? What makes you angry? What aspects of your behaviour can you control? What behaviour can't you control? What do you think makes you healthy, or ill? The truth is that you already know more than enough about yourself to make the decisions which can change your life. What you don't know about yourself, you can find out. You can read books, ask questions, experiment.

Doctors, priests, lawyers, bankers and hypnotherapists should be regarded as no more than advisers. What you do about your health is ultimately your own responsibility.

HypnoHealth is not an answer to all your ills. It's a road map for self-exploration, and a tool for you to use as you see fit. This book introduces you to the power of your own mind. It shows you how to turn that power into good health. Use what works; leave the rest. Health is not something that happens to you, it's something that you can create for yourself.

Let's start by being clear about the goal. Health means balance. Even the healthiest body is home to germs, viruses and a range of potential illnesses. What we call good health is nothing more than a balance between the things that can kill us and the things which keep us alive. Emotional health means enough emotional release to feel alive, but not so much you feel overwhelmed. Financial health means enough money so you don't have to worry about it, but not so much you become burdened. Spiritual health means enough faith to see you through, but not so much that you become fanatical. Health is balance in every area of your life: body, mind and spirit.

When some people think of balance, they think of a tightrope walker on a thin wire. But real health is like gently paddling a canoe downriver on a summer's day. It comes from a feeling of calm. Luckily, there is an entire *ocean* of calm inside your mind. You don't have to get, inject or swallow anything to create perfect health. Everything you need already exists deep inside your own inner or subconscious mind. Through hypnosis, you can tap into this reservoir to create your own healthy balance. Begin the journey to health by considering the source of your transformational power: your attitude.

Your attitude is what you tell yourself. Your attitude is your thoughts. *Nothing is more important than your attitude.* It's no exaggeration to say that it's the difference between life and death. Concentration-camp survivors will tell you about the men and women who saw suffering around them, fell into despair and perished. What about the well-paid executives who 'kick the bucket' within two years of retirement? Cut-off from their life's work, unable to find a reason to live, some ex-executives give up living . . . and die. A bad attitude puts a lifetime of stress on your heart and immune system. You literally wear yourself out.

But many people survive tragedy, find inner strength and go on to make something special of their lives. And not all retired executives endlessly mourn past glory. Once liberated from the shackles of their nine-to-five jobs, many older people find even better reasons to get up in the morning – from volunteer work to higher education. Have you ever wondered why some people live to be one hundred, while others never see their fiftieth birthday? What's the secret? What makes them thrive when others can't even survive?

Their thoughts.

Their attitude.

Your thoughts determine how you feel. If you tell yourself that you're constantly in danger; if you worry about the past or the future if you criticise yourself for being lazy, stupid or foolish; if you think about how terrible things are, you feel depressed. Miserable. Tense. Worried. If you feel depressed, miserable, tense and worried, your mind and body cannot function properly. Have you ever bumped into a piece of furniture because you were so preoccupied with something? It's a sign that you're not thinking properly. So is heartburn. And neck ache. And backache. And insomnia. And excessive drinking. And depression. And anxiety. Almost all mental and physical ailments can be linked to the way you think.

Try it the other way. If you tell yourself you can handle any situation; if you live for the moment, let go of the past and let the future take care of itself; if you constantly tell yourself you're more than good enough; if you stop and consider the positive side of even the most desperate situation, you feel calm. Relaxed. Positive. Happy. If you feel calm, relaxed, positive and happy, your mind and body function easily. Have you ever come up with a brilliant solution to a problem when you were doing something relaxing but completely unrelated? That's a sign that you're thinking properly. So is fitness. And a good night's sleep. And daydreaming. And happy times with close friends. And a supportive relationship. Almost all of life's mental and physical benefits can be linked to the way you think.

Researchers, scientists, doctors, alternative practitioners and patients are all exploring the connection between mind and body. Growing scientific evidence suggests that our thoughts are the single most important factor for creating health. Even so, it still comes down to belief. If you believe cancer is something that happens to you – not something you create or cure – you're not going to find much health inside your mind. If you believe you can change your body chemistry by the power of thought alone, you can. What you believe to be true, is true. If you believe something is out of your control, you're right. If you believe something is within your control, you're right.

MY ATTITUDE DETERMINES WHETHER I'M HAPPY AND HEALTHY, OR ILL AND MISERABLE.

If you agree to take this idea for a test run, you may have to abandon a lot of ideas about yourself and what happens to you. You can never have the comfort of seeing yourself as a victim. You can't simply surrender your mind or body to a doctor or therapist and say,

'That's it then. It's out of my hands.' Instead, you have to take responsibility for your situation, seek out advice, decide what to think, decide what to do, take responsibility for what happens, seek out more advice, make another decision, and so on. There's no sense of 'There, that's it. I'm healthy.' Only, 'What do I need to do today to *maintain* my health and happiness?' While it's frightening to sever the umbilical cord to the so-called experts, it's enormously liberating to discover your own personal power.

Hypnosis is a way to tap into that personal power. With self-hypnosis, you can change bad habits, unleash creative potential, explore hidden abilities and overcome obstacles. It's simply a matter of learning how to re-train your subconscious mind — the part of your mind responsible for all your habits and non-thinking physical responses (i.e., blinking, digestive system, muscle co-ordination, etc.). The techniques of self-hypnosis are so simple and effective that you can begin right now. Skip to Part Four and away you go.

Most people want to know why they have a problem before they attempt to change or overcome it. A lot of people — ninety per cent of therapists included — believe that knowing why a problem exists *is* the cure. To get the most out of self-hypnosis, you'll have to abandon that idea as well.

Although it might be interesting, you don't need to know why you have a problem to cure it. The hunt for self-knowledge is a fascinating adventure. 'Why' therapies like psychoanalysis may not be very effective, but they're never dull. If you want to find health and happiness, with a new lifestyle, explanations are not enough. You need to go deeper than rational thinking. You have to hypnotise the part of your mind that is illogical, irrational and often a bit slow: your subconscious mind.

Although the subconscious mind ultimately holds the key to health, the rational or conscious mind can definitely block your path. If the rational mind clings to old beliefs too strongly, it prevents you from making the deep changes which can alter your life. So you need to prepare your mind to accept new programming by examining the old. To create health, you have to re-define illness.

Once again, it comes down to a question of attitude. If you're ill or stuck in a bad habit, the chances are you've got what my games teacher used to call 'an attitude sickness'. I reached this conclusion after treating hundreds of clients. I began to see that specific problems are connected to the client's way of looking at things. Stressed executives tend to be perfectionists. They see life as a climb up an endless ladder. Arthritis sufferers have tremendous difficulty expressing their

emotions. They see life as a struggle against constant disappointment.
Clients who can't get to sleep often view life as a minefield. One wrong
step and they lose everything. Many overweight women see life as a
dog-eat-dog nightmare.

Clients don't come up with these attitudes on their own. They don't
sit down and say right, life stinks, it's getting worse, so I'd better get
chronic backache. They learn their attitude to life from society, parents, teachers and friends. Then they become the next victim. It's no
surprise that the men suffering from stress have fathers who died of
heart attacks. Or that chronic worriers are raised by chronic worriers.
Attitude sickness is a communicable disease. Negative thinking is
passed down from generation to generation.

In the beginning, when clients came to me with a problem, I simply
used the powerful hypnotic techniques taught to me during my training. However, I soon discovered that I achieve far better results when
I attack the client's attitude sickness first. In other words, I now guide
them to a new way of looking at the world before I attempt to trans-
form their life. Before I implant healthy patterns into their subconscious mind, I challenge their world view. More often than not, this
makes clients slightly uncomfortable. Most people want me to cure
their symptoms and leave their attitude to life alone. But it doesn't
work that way.

Part Two of the book details the 'seven deadly attitudes': fear, guilt,
apathy, doubt, worry, obsession and resentment. These are some of
the attitude sicknesses we inherit from family and society. They are
the road blocks standing between you and your health and happiness.

Confront these negative patterns. Check out new ways of looking at
your own thoughts. Listen to how others have overcome their bad attitudes. Open your mind. At the same time, make no mistake: analysing
your negative attitudes probably won't 'cure' you. All you're doing is
preparing yourself for deep hypnotic re-programming, in the same
way that a farmer ploughs a field before planting seeds. But whatever's wrong with you, these seven deadly attitudes are the most
important diseases you'll ever fight.

The Beata Bishop Story

When psychotherapist Beata Bishop meets a cancer patient, she has
two questions: 'Do you want to live?' then, 'Do you want to live unconditionally?' 'A lot of patients want to live,' Beata reports. 'But they
can't commit themselves to life without conditions. They say: "I want
to live, but not if I have to look like this, or live in pain."' If a cancer

patient chooses life without strings, Beata helps them fight. If the patient clings to ifs and buts, she makes it clear that the battle will be twice as hard. 'Unless you want to live unconditionally,' she warns, 'you may not make it.'

Tough talk, but Beata's been there. In 1979, she developed malignant melanoma and had a cancerous tumour surgically removed from her leg. In 1980, a second tumour appeared in her groin. Her specialist gave her six months to live unless she underwent further surgery. Feeling angry and betrayed, she fought back with the Gerson therapy. This nutritional approach requires thirteen freshly pressed organic juices, five coffee enemas and one crude liver injection per day. You must also eat enough organic food to feed three rabbit warrens. It's physically demanding, lonely and expensive. But it worked. Two years later, Beata was given the all-clear. Nine and a half years later, she's alive and well, and living in the UK.

Even though the Gerson therapy focuses on diet, Beata believes her attitude helped save her life. 'You may not be conscious of it but you're giving your body a set of instructions,' she says. 'If you give it one set of instructions – get well – it will do its best. If you give it a second set of instructions – Oh my God, get me out of here – the body is confused. You depress your immune system. It can't heal.'

While Beata seems a born fighter, she rejects the idea that people can't change their attitude. Sometimes it takes a crisis to help us grow out of old patterns. As Beata puts it: 'Confronting imminent death concentrates the mind wonderfully.'

_ Positive Thinking: Nothing to Sneeze At _

Helen Foster writes articles about health for *Woman's Own* magazine in the UK. The 23-year-old journalist covers everything from menstrual pain to depression. Just like a first-year medical student, she often experiences the symptoms of the problem she's investigating: 'When I wrote about cystitis, I had to go to the loo every half-hour. When I did backache, I felt stiff all the time.' In addition to her phantom illnesses, Helen used to suffer a sniffling nose and sneezing fits whenever she went to bed. The congestion kept her from sleeping and made her tired and irritable. Helen wouldn't use the steroid nasal spray prescribed by her doctor and only took antihistamines when she was desperate. When she contacted me for an article on hypnotherapy I suggested we tackle her 'allergy problem'.

Helen was sceptical but eager. 'I've always been into complementary medicine. You name it, I've tried it: spiritual healing, aura reading, past-life regression therapy and more. Still, I couldn't see how
hypnosis could stop me sneezing.' I explained to her that her subconscious mind controlled her physical reactions to stimulus, whether that
was dust on the pillow or a particular food. I could use hypnosis to tap
into her subconscious and command it not to respond to the bedtime
stimulus with sniffles and sneezes. First, we tried to discover exactly
what triggered the problem: diet, detergent, stress, whatever.
Unfortunately, she couldn't link her distress to anything specific.
Fortunately, Helen was highly hypnotic. So we gave it a go.

The treatment worked, but Helen dismissed it. 'If I thought about it,
I thought it was a coincidence. When the problem came back a few
weeks later, I called you. You told me I wasn't thinking positively
about it. So when it happened again I told the problem to go away,
and it did. I always believed people have the ability to cure themselves. But I had this idea in the back of my head that I couldn't do it. I
guess that's what stopped me.'

You might think Helen now accepts the power of positive thinking,
and the link between attitude and health. Not quite. 'Put it this way. If
negative thinking causes illness, then we're really in trouble.'

THE SEVEN DEADLY ATTITUDES

'Things do not change. We change.'
Henry David Thoreau

2
Fear

Most of us would like to boldly do what we've never done before. Some people long to tell their boss exactly what they think of his or her ridiculous ideas. Others dream of exploring an exotic country. Some imagine themselves jumping out of an airplane. Even if your desire for new experience only takes you as far as a cooking class, there's a little bit of the adventurer inside all of us. It's a part of ourselves we need to encourage. Seeking out new experiences keeps us young. Trying something new stretches our abilities. Accomplishing something new boosts self-esteem.

And yet there's a part of us that's scared. It would be great to confront the boss – provided he doesn't turn around and give you the sack. Exploring an exotic country would be a real adventure – if you don't catch a disease. Jumping out of a plane? Are you kidding? What if the parachute doesn't open? We consider breaking out of our routine, feel the fear and bottle out. The feeling of being frightened imprisons us. It's hard to escape.

Overcoming fear is one of life's most satisfying, growing experiences. But it's a personal decision. Are the benefits worth the risk? Everyone is afraid of parachuting, but most of us don't see the point of leaping out of an aeroplane. An astronaut sitting atop a million pounds of rocket fuel is certainly heading for the adventure of a lifetime, but you can be excused for preferring your sofa to the space capsule. If you do decide to go for it but somehow can't, then it's time to take a closer look at what's holding you back.

Fear is a learned response; we *learn* to be frightened. Our parents are our first teachers. In a famous experiment, researchers placed an eight-month-old baby about twenty feet away from her mother. The floor between the two had a section of transparent perspex; it looked as if there was a large gap in the floor between mother and baby. The mother called the baby to come over. When the baby neared the perspex gap, the mother put on a frightened expression. The baby would stop. When the mother smiled and encouraged the baby, the baby would crawl right over 'thin air'. In the thousands of encounters between parent and child, a child quickly learns what, when, where and how to be frightened.

All our early authority figures – teachers, doctors, vicars, scout leaders, etc. – programme us with fear responses. A simple comment from your art teacher – 'Don't play with that, you'll poke your eye out!' – can put you off scissors forever. A dentist who promises 'this won't hurt a bit', then re-defines pain with a shiny drill can create a lifelong fear of dentists. It's not all accidental, either. Many adults instil and exploit children's fears to make them dependent. A vicar who threatens naughty children with 'the wages of sin is death' makes himself seem powerful to a child who wants to grow up. How many teachers use the fear of detention to prop up their classroom dictatorship? Authority figures teach us that fear creates power – and powerlessness.

Friends also teach us about fear. When a group of friends calls you chicken because you hesitate to jump off a high diving board, you're forced to choose between your fear and loss of face. Sometimes the result is positive: we summon up our courage, jump and feel great. We go on to try new things. Sometimes the result is disastrous: we lose the respect we crave from our friends. If we 'chicken-out' often enough, we begin to lose self-respect. Whether or not you jump, the underlying message is the same: *Fear is weakness*. It's not enough to *feel* fear; friends teach us to fear it. Franklin Roosevelt (who said, 'the only thing we have to fear is fear itself') probably grew up with some dare-devil buddies.

Experience is the other great teacher of fear. Your parents don't need to hold your hand over a naked flame for you to learn to be afraid of fire. Sooner or later you'll experience the pain of a burn and figure it out on your own. Of course, both burns and fears come in varying degrees. Imagine you woke up in the middle of the night choking in thick smoke, realised your bedroom was on fire and barely made it to safety before your home burned to the ground. The experience could create such a strong fear of fire that you might not get a decent sleep for years. A single unpleasant event in your past can leave a lifelong legacy of fear. You may not even remember it because fear can remain long after the experience has been forgotten.

To conquer fear, you have to re-educate yourself. The first step is to recognise that fear is a perfectly normal emotion. If humans didn't have a natural fear response, our species wouldn't exist. Our ancestors would have strolled fearlessly around the plains of Africa until they were all eaten by wild animals. Fear is a valuable human instinct that we experience in reaction to the threat of injury, humiliation or disaster. It's your inner mind saying 'Hold on a second here, what if something goes wrong?' If you're afraid of something bad happening – flunking an exam, losing a contest, breaking a leg or looking foolish – it's not because you're weak or stupid or timid. It's because it *really might happen.* Even fears which don't make much logical sense, such as a fear of spiders, are quite reasonable to the part of your mind dedicated to your health and safety.

The next step is coming to grips with the worst case scenario. What exactly are you frightened of? What would happen if your worst fears came true? Would you survive? Of course you would. Well, maybe.

Some people regularly do things that could kill them: soldiers, pilots, stunt people, police, racing drivers and others. To keep fear in check, they too have to come to terms with the worst case scenario. They have to say to themselves, 'If something goes wrong, I'm dead. If I die, I die. It's worth the risk.' It's not about *confronting* your fears. It's a question of *accepting* them. You look at the bleakest possibility and tell yourself that you can handle it. Only then are you really ready to give it your best shot.

Anyone who says they don't feel any fear is either a very bad liar or a very boring person. The truth is that you can never totally 'conquer' fear. The best you can do is make peace with your fears and get on with life. By doing whatever you want to do, you may eventually lose your fear. You may even wonder what you were afraid of in the first place. But then it's time to try something new. And the chances are you'll feel some new fear. That's the way it *should* be. It's a sign that you're growing.

The Fear of Flying Course Strikes it Lucky

In Manchester, the Fear of Flying programme finishes with a flight to the Isle of Man. On one occasion, the weather was closing in. Captain Hughes decided to fly anyway; the clients had been building to this flight all day. As the plane came into land, the turbulence became extreme. The passengers remained calm – even when the jet was struck by lightning. After landing, an elderly participant congratulated Captain Hughes, 'That was fantastic. But don't you think the lightning was a bit much?'

For many people, even the thought of flying is a bit much. Since much of that fear is based on ignorance, the Fear of Flying programme begins with the theory of flight. 'There are a lot of myths and misunderstandings about flying,' Captain Hughes says. 'We try to address all their rational fears, one by one – their "what ifs". Some people think the plane will fall out of the sky if the engines stop. In fact, even big jets can glide a long, long way.'

Dr Keith Stoll soothes the flying phobics' inner minds with group visualisation, and then it's off to the airport. 'In a group of 100, about ninety will file on to the plane quite happily. Ten to fifteen need extra encouragement, and two to three don't make it. Once we take off, there's an almighty cheer.' The relief and pride after touch-down is even more enthusiastic. (Captain Hughes has had five marriage proposals so far.) Self-esteem soars, and new possibilities beckon. One intrepid participant wrote to say she'd flown to the Caribbean, booked a helicopter flight down the Amazon and shot the rapids in a rubber boat. For another, graduation meant finally visiting her grandchildren in New Zealand.

In six years, Captain Hughes and his team have helped over 6000 people overcome their fear of flying. His advice about dealing with fear is simply to confront it: 'Fear is like a barking dog. If you run from it it will bite you on the leg.'

Spiders in the Duvet?

Paul Pearce-Kelly didn't feel fear the first time he picked up a Mexican bird-eating spider. London Zoo's head keeper of invertebrates says he felt 'trepidation' when he placed the mouse-sized spider on his palm. Call it what you will, Kelly is familiar with the fear most people feel when they encounter spiders. Day in and day out, he sees visitors' shock, horror and disgust at his rare arachnids. Kelly believes this negative reaction is both unrealistic and understandable.

'I do think there is some kind of natural reluctance to come into contact with the beasties,' Kelly admits. 'Everyone gets a bit alarmed when they see something small with a lot of legs scurry across a duvet. But our culture reinforces the fear beyond all reason. I see school parties all the time. The teacher comes in, takes one look at a spider and says, "Yuck! Isn't that horrible! Let's go see the lovely Pandas." That's conditioning.'

Kelly recommends arachnophobes get to know their perceived enemy. Decide what it is you're afraid of. If you're scared a spider is going to run up and bite you, it's helpful to know it won't. You may also want to know there isn't a single recorded case of death by spider bite in the UK. And spiders don't live in duvets. Do enough homework and you may even develop an appreciation for the web-slingers.

'Spiders are one of the oldest species in the world,' Kelly reveals proudly. 'Spider silk is still being examined for its technological possibilities. Medical researchers are looking at spider venom to help stroke victims. Spiders also provide a great deal of aesthetic pleasure. They're a very popular pet.'

Even if they don't provide their offspring with a pet spider, Kelly thinks parents should ensure that children don't develop arachnophobia. That's why little baby James Pearce-Kelly has a plastic spider hanging over his cot.

_ Crime: Your Worst Fears May Be True _

When Rachel Nickell was raped and murdered on Wimbledon Common in front of her two-year-old son, the media called Shirley Tulloch. As inspector for the Metropolitan Police Community Affairs department, she asks for public information to solve crimes and offers sensible crime-prevention advice. She also tries to reduce fears by putting sensational crime into perspective. The message does not always get through.

'Random attacks like Wimbledon Common are extremely rare. Two-thirds of all rape victims know the offender. You are far more likely to be attacked at home. But that's not what the public wants to hear. They want to hear we have caught the rapist and he's a madman. They're thinking "My God, it's not even safe to walk in a park at nine a.m.!"'

Inspector Tulloch plays a strange dual role. On one hand, she is the official voice of calm. She reassures the public that crime is less common than the media would lead them to believe. 'I'll ask a group to stop and think who they know who's been dragged off the street and raped. Realistically, statistically, they are not likely to become a victim of violent crime.' On the other hand, Inspector Tulloch tries to raise public awareness to prevent crime. 'I don't think people are afraid *enough*. Until they lose a handbag or suffer a burglary or face an attacker, they don't take sensible precautions. They're afraid, but somewhere in the back of their mind they think it will never happen to them.'

In her sixteen-year career, Inspector Tulloch has dealt with child abuse, vice and terrorist bombs. She still conducts hostage negotiations. When it is time for her personally to confront violent crime,

Inspector Tulloch puts on her 'professional hat'. 'I'm quite calm and don't get excited. I only feel fear afterwards. As long as fear doesn't affect the quality of your life, a little bit is quite healthy. It keeps you sharp.'

3
Guilt

Guilt is what we feel when we believe we've done something wrong. It's the nagging, soul-destroying sense that we made a mistake we can't put right. Sometimes we can't. Many people spend their lives carrying a burden of guilt because they can't undo what's already been done. Sometimes we can put things right, but we'd rather live with the guilt than admit to ourselves or others that we were wrong. No matter what the facts are – whether you can make amends or only live with what you've done – guilt makes us feel weak and powerless. No fine, no jail, no physical pain is as debilitating as guilt. It's a useless emotion.

This is not a popular position. Society wields the weapon of guilt with full righteousness. It expects and demands guilt for a wide range of anti-social behaviour – from not paying your parking fine to murder. If someone commits a particularly brutal crime, it is considered only right and proper that the criminal should be condemned to life-long guilt, shame and remorse. Some go even further. They see guilt as the ultimate test of an individual's character and social responsibility. If you don't feel guilty for breaking society's rules, you don't belong in society. You're damned if you don't feel guilty, and you're damned uncomfortable if you do. In fact, you're paralysed. And that's the point. Society uses guilt to make individuals submit to authority. A paranoid fantasy? Take a look at guilt on the family level.

The stereotypical mother who manipulates her children with guilt has its roots in practical fact. If a child is convinced he or she can never make up for the parent's pain, suffering and sacrifice, the child will spend his or her whole life looking for forgiveness. The parent can withhold this forgiveness, offer it only on certain conditions or provide it in tiny doses. The parent also reserves the right to withdraw forgiveness at any time. It's emotional blackmail of the first order, and it's very effective. No wonder teachers, clergy, police, judges and most authority figures set guilt traps for anyone they want to control.

Rest assured, we all fall into these traps with alarming regularity. You can be sitting quietly at home watching a video when a little voice inside your head suddenly says your poor mother is all alone and miserable and sitting by the phone, waiting for your call. The fact that you were quite happy a second before and no one *really* sits by the phone makes no difference. You wonder when you last called home. It suddenly seems like forever – even though it might have been two days ago. Welcome to remote-control parental guilt.

Or imagine you've just been promoted. You're breaking the news to your co-workers. You worked hard for this promotion and you should feel great. But that little voice inside is saying maybe someone else deserves the promotion more. You feel a little sheepish as you recall all the times your work wasn't quite as good as it should have been, and those days off when you weren't really ill. You see the faces of your co-workers. Some don't share your happiness as much as they might. In fact, a few of them look downright resentful. You start to doubt yourself. After all, these colleagues must have *some* reason to feel jealous. Welcome to don't-get-ideas-above-your-station, always-know-your-place guilt.

It's worth making a distinction between guilt and regret. Regret is a rational reaction to a mistake. You look at what you've done and see that it was a bad move. If you realise you made a mistake, take responsibility for what happened, put right what you can and resolve not to repeat the same mistake again, you shouldn't feel guilty. You may feel regret, you may wish you'd never made the mistake in the first place, you may feel shame, but you shouldn't feel guilty. If you do feel permanently stained or somehow worthless, even *after* you've faced-up to your errors, there's something going on besides simple wrong-doing. It's usually a bad case of the 'born-guilty blues'.

Many children grow up in an environment where they are always criticised, never encouraged. They're constantly told they are defective. No amount of achievement is good enough. Some parents adopt this ever-critical approach out of misconceived love. Life's tough, so my kid should be toughened for life. Who better to do it than the person who loves them? Other parents are hard on their children because that's the way they were raised. 'If you think I'm tough, you should've seen my father. If I did something wrong he'd whack me into next week'. Some parents are cruel to their children because that's how they feel about themselves. The result can be devastating. All children are deeply impressionable. They can easily be led to believe that they are fundamentally bad. They can grow up with a deeply held belief that they're guilty simply for being alive.

To a greater or lesser extent, we all face the weapon called guilt. No one is completely immune to someone powerful who's determined to make others feel small and weak – especially if that 'someone' is themselves. To defend against guilt, you must delve into that part of your mind where the 'born-guilty blues' plays its dismal tune. Counselling, prayer, self-hypnosis and other types of therapy can help root out feelings of low self-esteem. You can then re-establish who you are and, more importantly, how you feel about yourself. Meanwhile, shelter behind a shield of reason, because guilt is not based on reason. By examining your own actions calmly and logically, you can step lightly over guilt traps and avoid self-inflicted wounds.

Ask yourself if you *really* did something wrong. Most people never question what they believe to be right or wrong. For example, most adulterers simply accept the concept that extra-marital sex is wrong and secretly suffer the sword of 'deserved' guilt. But a constantly unfaithful partner should look deeper. He should ask himself if *he* thinks he was wrong. If he honestly believes his extra-marital sex is justified, he should not waste time and energy feeling guilty. He should face the fact that he cannot or will not live up to his vows. He should re-evaluate his marriage, and change what needs changing. This kind of realisation – that you can't live up to accepted and expected standards of behaviour – is never easy. The fall-out is often painful and frightening. Yet living in perpetual guilt is worse.

It's surprising how often we feel guilty for something that's not our fault. The classic guilt-producing argument is, 'Your father and I slaved and suffered so you could be happy' or 'You almost killed me when you were born'. Reason is your only defence. Did you ask your parents to slave and suffer for you? When you were being born, did you say, 'Right, now I'm going to kill this woman'? You were not responsible. You are never completely responsible for how people react to you. If a co-worker is jealous of your success, it's not normally because you *made* them jealous. Remember, people have good reasons to believe you're at fault. They have even better reasons for convincing *you* that something is *your* fault. Always retain the right to decide for yourself.

Once you free yourself from guilt, you'll never need to depend on anyone for your self-esteem. If you admit your mistakes, make good and move on, you don't need someone else to prod your conscience. You don't need someone else to forgive you so you can finally 'live with yourself.' And you won't need to beat yourself up all the time. You can explore life's adventures knowing that no matter what happens, you'll take responsibility, learn and improve. That's all anyone can do.

—— Forgive Me, Father, for I Have Sinned ——

Father Columba Ryan, a parish priest in northern England, remembers a young man who regularly confessed to the sin of fornication – almost as soon as it happened. The man revealed his sexual exploits and asked for forgiveness. One day, Father Ryan refused to hear his confession. 'Confession is not a kind of psychiatrist's couch. Unless you say "I've done wrong *and* I will make amends *and* I will try to do better in the future", confession is worthless. Anything else is merely washing your face to get clean.'

Father Ryan thinks that many Catholics confess to try and rid themselves of 'bogus guilt'. For example, he recalls a young woman who felt guilty because she didn't do everything her elderly mother demanded. As bad as she felt, the daughter had not committed a sin. She had not poisoned her mother or in some other way turned her back on God. She had nothing to atone for. Father Ryan believes this type of irrational guilt – what he calls an FIF (funny inside feeling) – does not belong in the confessional.

Father Ryan is well aware that some religious teachers lay too much stress on guilt. 'Some of us are taught to believe that God is all goodness and they are bad and impoverished in the face of Him. They are brought up with a stronger sense of the fear of God than the love of God.' Father Ryan says there is no religious justification for this approach, which creates a niggling feeling of being guilty in spite of everything. 'Guilt and confession used as manipulation should be denounced. It is a total misuse of religious authority.'

Father Ryan believes the confessional is a valid model for Catholics and non-Catholics alike. 'If you genuinely love God, you want to make amends. If you are feeling guilty, share your burden with someone. It's always easier for two to carry a burden than one.'

—————— The Guilt of a Rapist ——————

Joe G. does not deny his crimes. Sitting calmly in a prison common room, Joe looks me straight in the eye and tells me that he robbed, raped and brutally beat a woman in March 1987. It was the second time. The first time, Joe served five and a half years in a traditional prison. This time around, he's serving a life sentence in G-wing, the sex offenders' unit of Grendon prison's 'therapeutic community'. Although Joe freely admits he's guilty as charged, he doesn't spend sleepless nights feeling guilty. In fact, he feels better about himself than ever. He realises his new peace of mind will not be welcomed on the outside.

'People want us to feel guilty all the time,' Joe says. 'They want us to suffer for what we've done. I do feel bad for the amount of violence I used. There was no reason for it. But guilt is like a bereavement. It wears off. You learn to shut it away. Is that a bad thing? I don't know, but I'd rather feel good than bad. If I feel good, I'm less likely to get into trouble.'

Grendon prison tries to reform prisoners like Joe through group and individual psychotherapy. It's the only prison of its type in the UK. The thirty-year-old 'experiment' hasn't really caught on because tax-payers are not buying Joe's argument that society benefits if he feels good about himself. Society wants criminals to feel bad. The desire to punish is far greater than the desire to reform. Joe is well familiar with that perspective.

'My Mum used to beat the hell out of me. She locked me in a cup-board if she thought I did anything wrong, and she *always* thought I'd done something wrong. Her beatings never made me feel guilty or stopped me from drinking and robbing and all that. All it did was make me angry. Instead of raping those women, I should have bopped her on the nose.'

Joe claims he wouldn't have raped again if he'd come to Grendon after his first offence. He says that in all of his forty-three years, he was never shown a better way to express his anger and fears. As for guilt, 'it doesn't keep me from doing things'. That's a disturbing thought coming from a violent criminal. On the other hand, if we want less violent crime, we may have to believe him.

'People on the outside don't understand that just because you're in prison doesn't mean you're being punished. I've been in and out of prison for thirty years. I've done time so often, prison doesn't hold any fears for me. It's the outside that scares me.'

4

Apathy

It's not always easy to get out of bed. Sometimes, it's tempting to just pull up the covers, snuggle down and let the world take care of itself. Even when you do manage to stagger into the bathroom, there are moments in everyone's life when starting something new – or doing the same old thing – is like trying to swim through peanut butter. Apathy can strike at the strangest times. You may be totally dedicated to a project, really looking forward to getting on with it, only to discover that playing with a rubber band is suddenly far more interesting than a long-delayed sales call. No one is totally immune to the virus called apathy, no matter how ambitious.

If you can't stick with something, don't immediately blame yourself. There are many good reasons for you to resist the urge. Remember that a great deal of everything we do in this life is deadly boring. Even racing-car drivers spend ninety per cent of their time doing things that have nothing to do with driving – getting to the track, preparing for the race and hanging around waiting for the start. Anyone who thinks movie stars lead lives of non-stop glamour and excitement should visit a film set. An actor can wait an entire day to speak two lines of dialogue. On a more ordinary level, most of us must spend a lot of time doing things that are less than inspirational: laundry, dishes, paying bills, getting to work, feeding ourselves, etc. All jobs and pursuits – from fighting fires to learning a foreign language – require a large amount of 'monkey work'. It's really no surprise that we often get bogged down with boredom.

Usually, we can get through the boring bits of any project by keeping the goal in mind. If you know you're going on holiday to France in six months, it's a lot easier to stick with your French lessons. If you can imagine the satisfaction of a clean house, it's easier to push the Hoover about. Although we're taught to see life as a series of steps leading to a goal, sometimes it's better to imagine the goal and work backwards in your mind. Close your eyes and see the job done. Feel the satisfaction and pride of achievement. Get excited. *Then* open your eyes and get on with the dull work that will take you where you want to go. Visiting your imagination to experience future pleasure is an excellent way to stay motivated.

Lack of motivation often comes from our early conditioning. When we're growing up, we're constantly told what will happen if we *don't* do something. When I was ten years old, my English teacher told the class that we'd never get into Harvard University if we failed our spelling tests. Years later, the football coach would describe in precise detail how ashamed we'd feel if we failed to beat our cross-town rivals. The threat of failure hangs over many a young life like a permanent rain cloud. And when you're always worrying about failure, imagining yourself *not* achieving, there's a little voice in your mind saying 'why bother?' Why bother doing something that probably won't work? Why bother doing something that may not be good enough? You might as well quit while you're behind. Nothing ventured, nothing lost.

It's not a productive or life-enhancing attitude. In fact, that type of negative thinking creates a vicious circle. You don't try anything new for fear of failure. You never try anything new, so your ability to solve problems withers from lack of use. When you do try new things, you're so out of practice, tense and nervous that you fail. Because you fail, you don't even want to try. Self-motivation disappears. If someone else tries to motivate you, you become hostile and angry. You're stuck in a rut.

Avoiding this 'why bother' trap requires a new motto: *'Failure is impossible'*. This is not American positive-speak, or a question of putting on rose-coloured Ray Bans. It's true. Look at it this way. How can you be perfect at something you don't know how to do? You can't. It's impossible. When you're learning – and we're *always* learning – mistakes are completely unavoidable. More than that, they are *vital* to growth and development. The only way to learn is through mistakes; an electric shock teaches a child to be careful with sockets. If you never made mistakes, you'd never learn, grow and develop. No matter how skilled someone seems, no matter how imperfect you may seem in comparison, remember that everyone has to make mistakes to achieve.

Why not see all your mistakes as learning experiences? Then the only 'failure' is to stop trying. So if you're in there, giving it even a little bit of a go, failure is impossible. And if failure is impossible, you can stop worrying about achievement and get on with the business of achieving. Use self-hypnosis to plant this message deep in your mind and the spectre of failure will never again haunt your ambitions. On the other hand . . . there are times when a positive outlook isn't enough to overcome apathy. That's when it's time to take a closer look at your inner mind and face some tough questions.

Apathy can be your mind's way of saying 'no thanks'. When it's really hard to stick with something, you may have to stop and ask yourself, 'Do I really want to do this?' Sure, your rational mind might think it's a great idea to learn how to play squash. It would be an excellent way to stay in shape and get in with some of the people in the company. But would it be any fun? Just because you *can* do something is no reason to do it. Is the thrill of speaking German worth hours of study? Is the promotion worth the hours of mindless drudgery? For some, yes. For others, no. When you can't get motivated, it's not always a bad thing to simply forget it and move on.

Society, parents and peers are all too ready to tell us what we should do. Pick up a woman's magazine and you'll see a hidden agenda: education, career, self-improvement, beauty, romance, babies. Look at your friends' lives and you'll see a remarkable similarity in skills, goals and plans. Turn on the television and see how many adverts portray a sexy, high-spending lifestyle. One of the real thrills of being an adult is the ability to say 'No'. Sometimes, you can sense straightaway that it's right to say no. No, I don't want to join the army. No, that dress isn't for me. Other times, the best way to tell if you don't want to do something is to try it out. Great test drive, but I don't want to buy this car. Make up your own mind. If you can't get motivated to do something and your life doesn't depend on it, drop it.

In the Star Wars movie *Return of the Jedi*, Luke Skywalker is learning to control the mystical power called 'the force'. Yoda, his teacher, tells Luke to raise his spaceship out of the swamp with the power of his own mind. Luke is more than a little sceptical. 'All right,' he sighs. 'I'll try.' His teacher becomes angry. 'No trying!' Yoda snaps. 'Either do or don't do. No trying!'

And that's the right way to look at motivation. When you want to do something, do it. When you don't want to do it, don't. The trick is to discover what you want to do. It's some trick! Knowing what you want to do in life at any given moment is the pursuit of a lifetime. So give yourself all the time you need to make up your mind, and reserve the right to change your mind. Only a fool worries about finishing a journey if he's not sure where he wants to go.

Dieters Hungry for Success

Within a few minutes of meeting a new weight-loss client, Dr Raj Subbarayan can pretty much tell if they'll succeed. In the last two years, the director of a diet clinic and healthcare centre has seen nearly a thousand clients. Her weight-loss programme includes a brief medical, an extensive review of the client's eating and exercise habits and a personalised diet plan. Despite Dr Raj's comprehensive and caring approach, she realises that only about half of her paying customers will ever make it to their target weight. The difference between clients who shed pounds and those who remain trapped by their habits is not will-power. It's motivation.

'Some clients come because they look in a mirror one day and they don't like what they see. Some want to lose weight because they're interviewing for a good job. Others are tired of spending money on bigger clothes all the time. Very few come for health reasons – they can't get up the stairs or feel ill. Most clients just want to look good in a swimsuit when they're on holiday. Summer is the boom time in the diet clinic business.'

Some of these reasons are more powerful than others, and you need powerful motivation to stay on a strict, calorie-controlled diet. Given the determination required, Dr Raj says successful clients must have a clear goal in mind. 'Women who want to lose weight to look good in a bikini tend to lose a bit, then give up when they find out how hard it is. Clients who are trying to lose weight for a wedding or a job interview almost always manage to stick with it. The key to motivation is to have a fixed goal in mind, then reward yourself for the achievements along the way.'

Dr Raj has learned to identify motivated clients by a number of subtle clues. They tend to be more enthusiastic. They really listen and try to understand her explanations and instructions. Most important, they've already imagined their success. 'They've already worked it out, exactly what they're going to wear and do when they lose the weight. They may lapse now and again, but their imagination keeps them going.'

Gotta Dance!

Stephen Jefferies is forty-one. In professional ballet, that's old, and Stephen knows it. The mind is still willing, but all too often the body is weak. The lead dancer's toes are not a pretty sight. Injuries and years of wear and tear have taken their toll. Even worse, the knives are out. Many people in the dance world would like Stephen to fail and retire from the stage. At this point in his career, Stephen has enough money and respect to make his living off-stage. But he can't. He's got to dance. As he rests between Saturday performances, he smiles and puts it simply, 'If I stop, I'll die.'

That kind of dedication may seem bizarre to non-dancers, but not to those who make their living in the ballet world. Ballet requires super-human discipline: class after class, leap after leap, day after day, year after year, performance after performance. It's a constant challenge with competition breathing down your neck every graceful step of the way. It took Stephen years of poverty, sweat, pain, criticism and end-less work to become a star. How in the world could anyone motivate themselves for so long, through so much? 'I just *had* to go to class every day. It was the only direction in my life. When everything around me was floundering, when I was in a mega-slump because my girlfriend left me, I could always lose myself in class. I could escape into the art form.'

That was then. Slowly but steadily, a different motivation has taken over. I think it's fear that keeps me going now. Fear of losing what I've gained. Even after all my success, I still have this anxiety people will take it all away. It's so easy to lose. If I stop exercising for one week, I can feel my body tightening up. I try to hold on by staying fit and doing well.'

Stephen is facing his off-stage future as positively as he can, training other dancers and taking comfort in the roles of husband and father. Looking back over his career, through injuries and accolades, disap-pointment and curtain calls, he has advice for people who find them-selves lacking motivation: 'If you lack motivation it's because you're doing the wrong things. People tell me they're doing a job they really hate. They shouldn't do it. If you're hanging on to a job just for the money, don't. Remember, no matter what happens, you will survive.'

5

Doubt

According to the gospel of St John, Jesus rose from the dead and appeared to his disciples the Sunday after crucifixion. One of Jesus's twelve disciples missed their master's visit. When Thomas heard the reports, he refused to believe Jesus had risen. Once he saw Jesus, once he touched Jesus's wounds for himself, *then* he would believe. A week later, Jesus appeared again to his disciples. This time, Thomas was there to see and touch his master's body. Even though his works earned him a sainthood, he was forever branded 'doubting Thomas'.

Today, when someone refuses to believe something others see plainly, the unbeliever is called a 'doubting Thomas'. They are said to be blind to the obvious, over-cautious, excessively critical, stubborn or just plain slow. Worst of all, they have no faith. Without faith, the logic goes, the doubting Thomas is condemned to a life of suspicion and indecision. Doubt is seen as anti-social, weak and pathetic. Yet, in a sense, we're all doubting Thomas.

Imagine you went into work one morning to hear your colleagues say 'you just missed the boss' – whose funeral you attended a week ago. You'd probably tell them to pull the other one, it has rosary beads on it. Granted your boss is not the Messiah, but most people would not take *any* life-after-death story on faith. Like Thomas, they'd want a bit more proof before changing their firmly held belief that the dead stay dead. And why not? Our concepts of truth and reality are built over a lifetime. They're critical to health and safety. If an African game-park ranger says lions are actually as tame as kittens, you'd still think twice about stepping out of a Land Rover with a ball of twine.

In fact, doubt is a fundamental ingredient of personal growth. People who take what they hear on faith and never question generally ,accepted 'wisdom', are usually trapped by their beliefs. I get many clients who hate their jobs. They suffer aches, pains, insomnia, boredom and stress. Often, I suggest they switch careers. Oh no, they couldn't do *that*. Not *now*. I'm too old, the economy stinks, and I'm not

trained for anything else. What do they base these depressing conclusions on? Not much. Certainly not on any attempt to find another job.
Maybe they *are* too old. Or maybe they're highly experienced. Maybe
their industry *is* depressed. Or maybe new opportunities are develop-
ing. Maybe their job skills *are* obsolete. Or maybe they translate well
into another area (e.g., taxi drivers make excellent computer program-
mers). Maybe is *always* better than *definitely not*.

We base our actions on set ideas about the world. This knowledge
of 'how things work' comes from an environment full of false or misleading information. For a start, can you really trust what your parents told you? Maybe they were wrong when they taught you life
lessons like 'What you don't know can't hurt you'. What about the
experts? Experts hardly agree on anything. When they do agree, it
usually doesn't last long. History is littered with abandoned theories
and ideas. What about your own experience? Consider the enormous
variety of human life. Then consider how few people, places and ideas
you've encountered. It's not terribly wise to draw general conclusions
based on your limited experience. Besides, we often believe what we
want to believe, rather than what our senses tell us. And our senses
lie. You can see something that's not there, or not see something that
is.

Confused? Good! When you're trying to change your life to find
health and happiness, you can't take anything for granted. You *need*
to doubt. Your firmly held beliefs could very well be the only thing
holding you back. With doubt, at least you're thinking about things in
a profound way. St Thomas didn't hear about Jesus's reappearance
and say, 'Rubbish!' and get on with his business. Nor did he say,
'Wow! Great!' and blithely get back to spreading the word. He
doubted. He prepared himself for a more profound and personal belief.
When someone tells you, 'That's not the way we do things around
here' or 'It'll never work', doubt them. People who accept what they're
told are open to manipulation. If Thomas believed everything told to
him on faith, he would have been susceptible to false prophets and
others who wanted to destroy the early church.

Of course, doubting the way the world works is one thing. Doubting
yourself is another. Or is it? If anything, our beliefs about ourselves
are even less reliable than our beliefs about the world. Our concept of
our abilities and basic worth is probably the most emotionally charged
area of our thinking. Self-knowledge is wide open to mistakes and misconceptions. When we're growing up, we normally accept someone
else's opinion of what we're good at, what we're bad at, and when
we're just plain hopeless. Our experiences then confirm these judge-

ments – or so we think. We soon begin to believe that there are parts
of our character we can't change. That's 'the way we are'. It's no surprise that some people can never seem to shake the lurking question
'Am I good enough?' Deep down, they're convinced they aren't.

I sometimes see young clients struggling with their studies. They're
convinced they're terminally 'weak' in a specific area, like maths.
Before I hypnotise them, I'll challenge their self-beliefs. Do you think a
brilliant teacher can make a student love a subject, whereas a bad one
kills it? If you love a subject, are you usually good at it? Have you ever
had a brilliant maths teacher? Can some students be really good at a
subject, but incredibly bad at tests? Are you any good at budgeting for
a new purchase, like a skateboard? So is it possible you could be good
at maths if you were motivated enough? I work to the same goal –
implanting a seed of doubt – with smokers, weight-loss clients and
clients who can't sleep. Maybe you *can* give up smoking, lose weight,
sleep soundly. You just haven't learned *how*. Yet.

Seen properly, self-doubt can be liberating, rather than imprisoning.
It can set you free. All you have to do is doubt your own self-doubt.
Begin to see your ideas about yourself as fluid, subject to change and
endless experimentation. Maybe you'll always be unhappy or addicted
or overweight or stupid or poor or lonely. Maybe not. To prepare the
field for the seeds of change, remove expressions of personal certainty.
Don't say 'I'm not the kind of person who . . .' or 'I'm really bad at . . .'
or 'I can never seem to . . .' or 'I'll always be . . .'. How do you know?
Maybe by saying those things to yourself, you're making them true.
You'll never *really* know if you can change something until you try.

Maybe doubt is the path to the rich, rewarding, open-ended life of a
true saint.

Hypnotic Breast Enhancement?

One autumn, Mary heard me claim on television that I could make
women's breasts bigger by tapping into the power of their inner mind.
She doubted it. The former ballet dancer didn't doubt hypnotic breast
enhancement could be successful – she believed in the power of the
subconscious mind. She doubted herself. 'I've always been like
Blanche DuBois in the play *A Streetcar Named Desire*,' Mary says. 'All
my life, I've thought if I want something too much, I can't have it.'
Even though Mary gave the technique less than a fifty–fifty chance,
she decided to go for it. Her doubts weren't as great as her dissatisfac-
tion with her own body. She felt unattractive and unfeminine. She

wouldn't go swimming, undress in a changing room, or look in a mirror.

In twenty-five hypnosis sessions, over seven months, Mary worked her way down to the deepest levels of trance. Once there, she imagined warm towels on her breasts, pictured herself just the way she wanted to be, commanded her endocrine glands to secrete growth hormones, revisited puberty – every technique I could find. Mary also devoted twenty minutes per day to self-hypnosis. Slowly but surely, her breasts began to grow. There were setbacks. Immediately after her period, the size of her breasts decreased slightly, and she had to climb back on track. Over all, Mary created a two-inch increase in her bust size, with no change in body weight. Even then, she had her doubts. She says it's no surprise her doubts are stronger than facts, considering her upbringing.

'Obviously, I wasn't born with doubt. As I grew up, my parents were always calling me names: ugly, stupid, horrible, slag, you name it. Nothing was ever good enough. When my father left us, I began to believe I could never get what I wanted in life. Certainly not the unconditional love I needed. So I became this person with a desperate drive for achievement on one side, and crippling self-doubt on the other. I could never relax. In a way, I became the doubt. It was so fundamental to my life that I saw everything else in relation to it. It ruled my life. When doubt rules your life, you feel paralysed.'

By taking control of her body and willing her breasts to grow, Mary had taken a giant step away from her feelings of powerlessness and self-doubt. Yet she rejects the idea that you can simply hypnotise away deep-seated feelings of low self-esteem. As far as she's concerned, doubt is an enemy that requires a long campaign. 'Self-doubt doesn't just go away. You have to confront it again and again and again. The key is to keep trying. Keep telling yourself that life's too short to say "I'd like to but I daren't." Eventually, it's got to get easier.'

The Doubts of a Mastermind

Stephen Allen was up against it in 1991. That year he earned a pittance as a professional actor. Added to his social security, it was hardly enough money to keep his family afloat. On the positive side, he had lots of time and little to lose. He decided to put his sponge-like memory to good use, and entered British TV's 'Mastermind'. The quiz show accepted his entry. While boning up on the life of Henry VII, Steve tried to control the doubts lurking in the back of his mind: 'It was a rough year, and I wasn't feeling too good about myself. I think I was able to push the doubts away partly because of tenacity, partly because of my training. As an actor, you learn to accept your doubts, realise that they're there, absorb them and come to terms with them.'

Steve found his first appearance on 'Mastermind' a particularly bizarre and demanding performance. 'There you are, alone in *the chair*, blackness all around, answering questions from a man who's god, father, host, interrogator, judge and jury all rolled into one. Talk about doubt! You begin to doubt the existence of your own physical body. You've simply got to concentrate and clear your mind enough to get on with it.' And so he did, winning the first round. Victory didn't increase his confidence. In fact, Steve's doubts grew worse. 'The more success I had, the greater the doubt became. I thought I must be heading for a fall. I just wouldn't allow myself to think of the possibility of winning. Not until the last question.'

After countless more hours studying Dartmoor National Park and the life and voyages of Sir Francis Drake, after answering the last question correctly, Steve emerged the overall winner. He was the BBC Mastermind of Great Britain, 1991. The win boosted his self-confidence and his profile, leading to work writing corporate videos, lecturing in performing arts and other drama-related work. Steve says the return to a more secure financial situation was welcome, but not the most important point. 'I measure success in spiritual terms. "Mastermind" taught me to see a crisis as a positive learning experience. If you do the best you can and be honest about that, that's a measure of achievement in itself. I mean, success and failure are such hard things. There's a measure of each in each other. '

Suzy Lamplugh's Mother

When estate agent Suzy Lamplugh disappeared without a trace in 1986, the public was beside itself with doubt – and fear. Who was the man she had agreed to meet? Why was her car found undisturbed? Who had pushed the passenger's seat back? Where was she? Had she been kidnapped? Had she left the country? Was she alive or dead? One person who didn't have any doubts about Suzy's well-being was her mother, Diana Lamplugh. 'From the moment I heard that she was missing, I knew something horrible had happened. As the weeks went on and on, I couldn't believe that she wouldn't respond to the press. I had the awful feeling throughout that we might never see her again.'

Six years later, Mrs Lamplugh is certain that her daughter is gone. 'I have no doubt at all that Suzy's dead.'

In those years, Mrs Lamplugh has tried to make sense of her family's tragedy. She founded the Suzy Lamplugh Trust to help give meaning to her loss. Through the trust, Mrs Lamplugh campaigns for public safety, such as demanding police supervision of the mini-cab industry. Two years after her daughter's disappearance, the police revealed that Suzy had been approached repeatedly by a known sex offender. When Mrs Lamplugh discovered the man's criminal record, she began to doubt the wisdom of the British penal system. 'I went off to find out what kind of world would let out a sex offender who was known to be very dangerous, and was suspected of raping forty-one women and murdering three others.' The trust now lobbies for tighter control over the parole system, treatment of sex offenders and increased monitoring and supervision of criminals after their release.

Although Suzy's disappearance has forever changed Mrs Lamplugh's vision of the world, a strong faith helped her through her painful education. 'I have always believed that life is pretty good. . If I kept feeling sorry and distressed about what happened, it would be self-indulgent. The rest of my family didn't need that. Suzy's dead, and she doesn't need that.' Mrs Lamplugh never questioned her beliefs – until the publication of a book about Suzy. 'The book basically indicates that I pushed her too hard, that what happened to Suzy was my fault, that my work was self-serving and insincere. I couldn't help but think it must be true.

The book sent Mrs Lamplugh into a six-month tailspin. She contacted Suzy's friends, to see if the author's version of events was true. Mrs Lamplugh was plagued with self-doubt. 'I kept asking myself, did I push my daughter to her death? Should I be putting myself in front of the public? Am I anything? I threw myself into writing a book about health and safety. But it wasn't until I went and saw a friend who happened to be a psychiatrist that I began to come to terms with myself. That's the toughest part: recognising yourself and deciding well, it's not perfect, but I can live with it.'

6
Worry

Worry is a cancer of the soul. It eats away at the human spirit until you're left with nothing but disappointment and misery. Worriers are perhaps the highest risk group for all major illness, from heart attack to cancer. They put enormous strain on their mind and body. People who expend most of their mental energy worrying not only shorten their own lives, but also the lives of the people around them. They create an atmosphere of constant danger and tension that pollutes any human endeavour.

Real worry – the kind of thinking that kills joy and maims happiness – is looking into the future and focusing on what could go wrong. Call it a pessimistic attitude or (as a pessimist would say) 'simply being realistic'. Whatever you call it, worry is pure, lethal, negative thinking.

There are plenty of good reasons *not* to worry. Free your mind from negative thoughts about the future and you free up mental energy. You can then use that energy to change the future, rather than worry about it. You'll get more done; earn more money; be more powerful. Eliminate worry from your life and you'll relax. You'll sleep more soundly, improve your digestion, increase your confidence, maybe even laugh a bit more. Your friends and family will like you better. Adopt a worry-free lifestyle and you'll have an excellent chance of baby-sitting for your great grand-children. Sold? If you're a hard-core worrier, probably not.

Like all our deeply held attitudes, worry is an inherited condition. Anyone who can remember their mother saying, 'Put your coat on! You'll catch your death!' has been programmed to worry. Many childhoods are filled with endless pronouncements from authority figures saying, 'If you don't . . . you'll . . .' If you don't study, you'll flunk. If you don't stop smoking, you'll get lung cancer. If you don't go out more, you'll never get married. Authority figures *could* say, 'Think how much better it will be when . . .' Think how much better it will be when you pass your exams, stop smoking, get married, save the planet, jail the pushers and make peace. But no, threats are supposedly more effective than inspiration.

This worrying mind-set is based on the idea that the world is a minefield. You can't be too careful. Worriers insist that they're simply anticipating what could go wrong. Then they can either avoid the problem or deal with it effectively. Why not prepare for the worst? Life is full of disappointment, danger and disaster. It's a seductive argument, and it makes sense – to a point. True, life isn't a bowl of cherries. If you're breathing, you're going to encounter disappointments, heartache and misery. Only a fool would deny that bad things happen to good people. The fatal flaw in this 'prepare for the inevitable' argument is that *worrying doesn't change anything*. In fact, it makes things worse.

One of my clients started a computer consultancy business in the depths of the recession. He was sleepless with worry. Before hypnotising him to relax, I asked him why he was so tense. For ten minutes, he explained what would happen if he didn't land his first customer. Bottom line: he'd end up on the street with no future. Fair enough, I said, that could happen, but why worry about it? Does dreading something stop it happening? Worrying was making him tired and nervous – not exactly the best frame of mind to impress potential customers. Why not think about how great it will feel to get that first sale? At least that way you can relax. And when you're relaxed, people relax with you.

One of the best arguments *against* worrying is the argument *for* positive thinking. Think positively about the future and positive things happen. It creates good luck in a practical and down-to-earth way. For one thing, people are more receptive to your ideas when you're unworried, calm and centred. For another, an unworried person is more attuned to life's possibilities. Worry about the future and you're lost in a cloud of depression. Think positively about the future and you're alert to opportunity. You find good luck.

I discovered how this works when I interviewed for a TV producer's job. The interviewer and I had very different ideas about the proper role of TV journalists. He seemed to think reporters had a duty to interview people who'd just lost their loved ones in horrific accidents. We ended up literally yelling at each other. Leaving the interview room, I had every reason to be depressed about my prospects. I really needed a job, and there was nothing else on the horizon. Instead of slinking off and sinking into gloom, I told myself not to worry. I spent a few minutes calmly warning the next interviewee what to expect.

The applicant gave me his card and thanked me for the inside info. We stayed in touch. A year later, he hired me.

Contrary to popular opinion, positive thinking about the future doesn't mean mindless optimism. It means adopting a balanced, realistic attitude to events. If the bank is about to foreclose on your house, you don't simply shrug your shoulders and say, 'No problem. I'm sure it will all work out.' By all means prepare for the worst. But think positively to relax. The more relaxed you are, the easier it will be to find a way out. Although the captain of the *Titanic* had every reason to be optimistic about the safety of his vessel, he still should have checked the waters. There's nothing wrong with keeping an eye out for submerged icebergs, and having plans to deal with them.

Scanning and planning for failure when the cost of failure is high is 'justifiable concern'. To succeed in life, to find health and happiness, you need a balance between concern and thinking positively. It isn't easy. Generally speaking, the less you have to lose, the less you need to worry. The trick is to put your problems in perspective. Most of the dangers lurking out there aren't really all that dangerous. Think about how many times your worst fear came true and it wasn't so bad. You survived, didn't you?

In a way, bad luck and mistakes actually make us stronger and wiser. Anyway, since you can't know what the future holds, why spend all your time and energy preparing for something that might never happen? Better to enjoy life moment by moment and let the future take care of itself.

A Mother Worries

'Sometimes, I feel like gathering my children around me and never going out the front gate.' Like most mothers, Gillian Aldam worries about the safety of her children, James (ten) and Kate (fourteen). Unlike many mothers, Gillian is a stunt woman. She's leapt seventy feet out of a moving cable car into eight feet of water (*Where Eagles Dare*), nearly died after a fight scene on a moving train (*The Wrecking Crew*) and perfected the fine art of driving a Russian truck through a forest at sixty miles per hour (*The Looking Glass War*). Yet Gillian still wakes up in the middle of the night in a blind panic, worrying about her children hurting themselves. At times like these, she uses her stunt training to ease her mind.

'Stunting has taught me how to cope,' she says. 'I've learned to control the emotions so they don't run away with you. Whether it's a long fall off a tall building or thinking about James riding his bike on public roads, I mentally talk myself through the fears. I tell myself to look at things logically and rationally. It's hard, but I *have* to let go of my children. Otherwise, they'll never do anything. After all, my worrying isn't going to stop anything bad happening. It might actually *make* it happen; like people who are so afraid of being ill, they become ill.'

This kind of mind-over-emotion trick requires a strong character. Although no one who's seen her work would accuse Gillian of being weak-willed, a good deal of her character was forged by her husband's death. John Crewdson was a first-class pilot who pioneered aviation stunt work and cinematography. When he died in a helicopter crash, Kate was only four and James was twenty-four weeks old. Gillian admits that trying to cope as a single mother has added to her worries. 'If my husband was alive, I'd have someone to share my worries with. As it is, there's no respite from my concerns, no space to relax. My children are all I have in this world.'

So why does Gillian continue her stunt work? Surely she must be worried about making her children orphans? 'When I go off to work, I have to put thoughts about the children on the back burner. I know that sounds cold, but if I don't concentrate fully on what I'm doing, something could go very wrong ... I stunt because I need the money, and I love it. I suppose that's the most important lesson I have to teach my children: Do what you love to do. I can't let my worry get in the way of their happiness.'

Keeping the Peace Within: How a Policeman Handles the Job

Sergeant John Moran doesn't worry about his personal safety. After two tours in Ireland with the army and eleven years with the police constabulary, the muscular 35-year-old can handle violent situations. Whether it's subduing a wife-abusing drunk, or preventing five thugs from beating up a young boy in a pub car park, Moran has faced physical danger and not been found wanting. *After* the danger has passed, it's another story. 'I always go over it in my mind,' Moran says. 'I worry, did I do that right? Could I have done it better? Sometimes, I mentally tear myself apart.'

Moran also experiences a more powerful, long-term concern that's always in the back of his mind: loss of control. Like all police officers, he routinely faces high-voltage aggression and animosity. Yet the men and women in blue don't have the luxury of releasing their anger or frustration on the general public. They have to grin and bear it. Moran

vents his aggression and adrenalin after the event by lifting weights or
going for a run. Sometimes, it's not so easy to 'save' his feelings until
later . . .

'I saw this chap driving a mini-bus, holding a mobile phone. The
bus was wandering all over the road. The driver pulled over to let six
kids out for school. Six kids who could have been killed because he
didn't pay attention. So I go over to have a word. Immediately, the
driver became abusive, denying it ever happened, personally attacking
me, using foul language. Somehow I managed to keep my cool, but I
kept thinking, if I wasn't in uniform . . . My worst worry is that I'll lose
it, get charged with assault and lose my job. I'll also lose my self-
respect. As a police officer, I should always be in control.'

Sergeant Moran now spends most of his time supervising eight
patrolling officers. He's developed a technique to deal with the worries
of supervising others. 'Before I talk to one of my PCs, I sit down in a
quiet place for about ten minutes with a cup of coffee and imagine
what will take place. I plan out what will happen if I say this or that. I
think, what's the worst scenario? Then I go over my first few words a
few times. As long as I don't over-extend it, it helps release the tension. It gives me that extra degree of confidence, so when I go into the
situation I feel like I'm in charge of what's happening.'

The only other worry that Moran occasionally experiences is worry
about the performance and safety of his men. That's one problem he
bears with pride. 'That's what I get the extra money for,' Moran says
with a smile. 'That's why I've got these stripes on my shoulder.'

7

Obsession

Think of all the things you do in the course of a lifetime. What do you do most? Let's say you work a nine-to-five job for forty years. That's about 75,000 hours of work. Which is nothing compared to the 215,000 hours of sleep you may enjoy. When you're awake, you speak, so figure roughly 400,000 hours of communication per lifetime. But the thing you do most is think. No matter where you are or what you're doing, you're thinking. Even while you sleep, the inner part of your mind is active. The mind works twenty-four hours a day, seven days a week. That's a tremendous amount of energy. If you become obsessed – if your mind gets stuck in a repetitive pattern – your own mental energy can literally drive you crazy.

That's not to say all people with obsessions are crazy. Obsession simply means constant and intense mental focus. The absent-minded scientist who forgets to put on his trousers is a good example. Exactly how much mental focus is 'normal' and how much is 'obsessive' is open to debate. Someone who can't understand why people hang out at airports watching jets take off and land is quick to call all plane-spotters obsessive. The plane-spotting fraternity makes finer distinctions; there are weekend spotters and spotters who live to spot. Drawing the line between 'totally dedicated' and 'clearly obsessive' is nearly impossible, especially if you're a full-time plane-spotter. That kind of obsessive probably prefers to describe him- or herself as 'happy'.

Whether or not you're obsessed, and whether or not it's a problem, is ultimately your own decision. Soccer nuts, opera buffs, Elvis fans, ballet dancers, teenagers in love, train-spotters and the like should all feel free to explore the limits of their single-minded enthusiasm without worrying about ignorant cynics. However, mental focus *can* get dangerously out of control. There are times when people find themselves constantly thinking about something they don't want to think about. The person's mental energy gradually focuses on a smaller and smaller area – an area where answers always seem just beyond reach. It's the mental equivalent of a broken record, and its effects can be devastating.

Anorexia and bulimia are two all-too-common examples. I've treated both types of food obsession with hypnosis. More accurately, I've treated anorexia and bulimia with *de*-hypnosis. Women with eating disorders are already in a trance. They concentrate so much on food, eating and weight that they can't – or won't – think of anything else. My job is to distract them away from weight, calories, body image and other food issues. First, I work to convince sufferers that there's no 'answer' to their eating problem. There's no perfect weight that can be achieved with their current eating habits. Then we discuss what else they have in their life besides food: their hopes, dreams, plans, friends, interests, etc. Finally, if they're ready, I try to introduce a normal, natural eating pattern. With a little inspiration and some deep hypnosis, their mind may let go of the obsession.

It's not very surprising that many people fall into obsessions. They begin with a goal or a dream. They invest a tremendous amount of mental energy and self-esteem in achieving the goal. When they find they can't make it, they conclude there must be something wrong with them (especially if someone else has succeeded before them). The feelings of self-doubt and self-loathing are intolerable. So they try again, and again. Every failure makes success seem more important. Every new attempt to 'figure it out' gets more and more desperate. Life becomes an epic struggle to achieve the goal. Inner panic sets in. Complexity disappears. If the rest of the world looks a little too hard to handle, the tendency to focus narrowly becomes even worse. The mind can only take so much self-abuse before collapse. The dream becomes a nightmare.

I had a young client whose goal was to let go of the past. She claimed she no longer loved her boyfriend and would have a much fuller life without him, but she wasn't sure. We explored the issues for four weeks without progress. I soon realised hypnotherapy was feeding her obsession with the relationship; it gave her another audience for horror stories about her boyfriend. When I attempted to switch the focus to her family and career, she became angry, sullen and withdrawn. She said, 'I feel there's no point to anything.' In the next session, she told me she had resorted to violence. Still, she was not ready to let go. She couldn't. After all, what else was there? A traumatic love life is better than . . . nothing.

Western society doesn't teach us how to let go. From the earliest age, we're taught achievement is all. And the only way to achieve is to strive. We're supposed to fix our minds on a goal and go for it. If we fail, it's our fault. Not achieving equals not trying hard enough! The truth is, humans can only achieve their full potential when they're relaxed. Many excellent students never make it to higher education because they can't handle the pressure of exams. First-class athletes are beaten again and again by competitors who can sleep peacefully the night before a big event. Peak performance requires relaxed concentration. But, how many schools include courses on meditation, self-hypnosis or any other type of relaxation? How many bosses say 'Your work isn't up to scratch lately, so take the afternoon off and get a massage'?

The same process of narrowing focus can affect entire societies. Nazi Germany is perhaps the most frightening example of a people ruled by its leader's obsessions. Devastated by inflation and war, German citizens were all too ready to exchange their weariness with life's complexities for Hitler's single-minded hatred of Jews and foreign 'enemies'. But Germany has no special claim to mass obsession. Throughout the world, the news media creates and feeds public obsession. We're bombarded with words and images about a particular story – usually violent and depressing – for days or weeks. The pressure builds and builds for us to 'do something', even when patience is the best solution. This manic obsession sometimes leads to a complete waste of personal and social energy, sometimes to war.

The danger of the media is not its message, but the amount of people who depend on that message for their sole understanding of the state of the world. Avoiding or eliminating obsession means widening your horizons. Society's health depends on its citizens exploring a free market of ideas and visions, both positive and negative. The danger of intense mental concentration is not what happens when we're concentrating, but how long we spend in our own little world. Personal health depends on pursuing an ever-changing variety of interests, pursuits and passions.

To remove or sidestep harmful obsessions, seek out new ideas and experiences in all areas of your life. Above all, you must learn to relax. Try to keep your problems in perspective. As they used to say at Cable News Network, 'Relax, it's not brain surgery.'

A Model Transformation

In the swinging Sixties, Celia Hammond had it all: beauty, fame, money and a non-stop social life. Then, one day, the world-famous photographic model passed a derelict house. An abandoned cat stared at her from a cracked window. Celia went home, but the image haunted her. So she returned to the house with a couple of friends. They broke in and found the cat trapped in a room with three dead kittens. After adopting the cat she called 'Jenny', Celia developed a reputation for rescuing cats. Soon, she had fifteen or sixteen felines in her flat. Her life changed completely. 'When I stopped turning up for jobs, when I turned my back on all that money, I knew I was dedicated. Once I started on that slippery slope, it just took over my life. Now I can't stop.'

Twenty-seven years later, you'll find Celia Hammond sitting alone in a van in an urban alleyway, waiting hours to trap feral cats. Or you may find her at her animal sanctuary in the British countryside, helping care for over 200 rescued cats, and numerous dogs. You *won't* find her posing for cameras, socialising at parties, taking a vacation, raising a family, decorating her house or anything else which detracts from her mission. Yet she rejects the idea that she dedicated her life to animal rescue because she enjoys it. 'My life is miserable. I'd rather be in a hot bath, or sitting in bed with a hot cup of coffee watching TV. I get cold, hungry and very, very tired. But I know there are cats out there who are cold and haven't got enough to eat. I don't have a normal life, but *someone's* got to do it.'

Some people still think Celia's mad for giving up a well-paid, exciting life for animal welfare. She's no stranger to the label 'obsessed'.

'Personally, I don't care what people call me. But I don't like the word; it smacks of lunacy. At this point, I simply can't afford to be taken for a pathetic figure because of my work . . . but I suppose I am obsessed. I'm obsessed about animal suffering, and the fact that if I try hard enough, I can do something about it. I'm obsessed with finding a long-term solution to the problem. That's why I'm going to get cheap spaying clinics if it's the last thing I do.'

If the RSPCA and the veterinary establishment relented in their opposition to cheap neutering, Celia Hammond believes she wouldn't have to 'scrab around railways looking for cats'. She's well aware that her rescue work is treating the symptom, rather than the cause. Wouldn't her time be better spent on the political front? 'I know I'm fiddling while Rome burns,' Celia admits. 'But I can't *not* do this [rescue animals]. I don't know why. Why does a junkie take drugs? I *have* to do it. If I don't do it, it won't get done.'

Watching the Juggernaut Go By
____ Obsessive–Compulsive Behaviour ____

Dr Paul Salkovskis is not bothered by train-spotters, love-smitten teenagers or Harley-Davidson fanatics. He considers that kind of person 'enthusiastic'. The senior research fellow at Oxford University treats people with obsessive–compulsive disorder. These are people plagued by unwanted, intrusive thoughts; thoughts which compel them to do something to stave off disaster. They can't fight the endlessly recurring negative thoughts and resulting behaviour. 'Let's say you're scared of a gas explosion,' Dr Salkovskis explains. 'Even though you know the gas is off, you keep wondering if the house is going to blow up. So every five minutes, you go and check the gas. You can't stop the thought, and you can't stop checking the gas. The same would apply to a religious person who can't stop blasphemous thoughts, and spends his or her entire day praying for forgiveness.'

Dr Salkovskis stresses that the difference between an obsessive–compulsive and a 'normal' person is not the thoughts themselves, but the person's reaction to them. 'Most people who stand on a train platform may at one time have thoughts about throwing themselves in front of the train, or pushing someone else on to the rails, or impulsively kissing a stranger. Most of us simply ignore these thoughts. The obsessive–compulsive simply can't let it go. The 'bad' thought feels so alien or unpleasant that they believe they must do something to neutralise the thought.

'But when exactly do "bad thoughts" become obsessive? When do sensible precautions become compulsive behaviour? . . . there's no strict dividing line between normal and obsessive.'

Although obsessive–compulsive disorder is extremely rare, it's difficult to cure. Up until the last fifteen years or so, treatment was drastic. Thousands of obsessive–compulsive patients had the frontal lobe of their brain surgically removed (lobotomy), or the connections to their frontal lobe burned off with an electrically charged wire (leucotomy). These operations were intended to sever the connection with the part of the brain that responds to the obsessive thought.

Fortunately, the medical establishment has all but completely backed away from this morally suspect approach. Today, people with obsessive–compulsive disorder are treated with drugs and/or therapy. 'One treatment is behavioural,' Dr Salkovskis says. 'If a patient is afraid of a gas explosion, we get them to leave the gas on at a low level and go out for a few minutes. The idea is to expose them to the "truth" of their negative thoughts, to show them they don't need to take a neutralising action.

'We also work on a cognitive level. I try to convince patients that they're trying to control the uncontrollable. A helpful idea to convey is that their negative thought is like a juggernaut coming down a motorway. If you step out in front of it to try and stop it, you get flattened every time. A much better solution is simply to stand by the side of the road and watch the juggernaut go by. Obsessive–compulsives have to learn simply to let negative thoughts go by. We *all* have negative thoughts. Really, the best way to control obsessive thoughts is to realise that no control is necessary.'

8

Resentment

Imagine you have everything you've ever wanted. Imagine yourself in the perfect job (or no job at all). See yourself living in the ideal home: large, comfortable rooms, swimming pool, huge garden, a gleaming car or two in the drive, whatever. Bask in the warmth of the perfect family: beautiful wife or handsome husband and loving kids. Bored? Pack your cases for a first-class trip to somewhere terribly exotic and wonderfully warm. Glowing good health, pots of money in the bank, love everywhere. Now imagine that it all belongs to someone else. How do you feel?

It's easy to feel resentment. All you have to do is think of something you want, then think of someone who's already got it. If you want to burn with envy, ask yourself if the person who's got what you want deserves it as much as you. To really be consumed with jealousy, try and figure out how you've been cheated from getting what you want. Never mind slippery slopes. Resentment is a fast-burning fuse straight to self-immolation. It's the kind of thinking that creates a raging inferno of bitterness, which destroys health and happiness from the inside out. Self-destruction may come as a heart attack, ulcer, alcoholism, domestic violence or depression and loneliness, but come it will. There is no such thing as healthy resentment.

There is no need to feel resentment. Just because someone else has what you want is no reason to hate them. In fact, you should welcome other people's achievement. If someone else can do something you want to do, the chances are that you can do it, too. To achieve the same thing for yourself – whether it's a mansion in Marbella, a body like Cindy Crawford's or the inner peace of a Tibetan monk – think like they think. See the world like they see the world. Do what they do. If it worked for them, it will probably work for you. Why re-invent the wheel? And why get stressed at someone else's success? See their accomplishments as a guidepost, not a roadblock.

Easier said than done? Probably. Overcoming resentment means overcoming a basic instinct: the urge to compete. Ever since early man first dragged his knuckles on the African savannah, individuals have tried to prove their value to the group. Nothing demonstrates self-worth to a group like competition. While this competitive spirit has taken us out of the trees and into the tower blocks, it also tends to separate humans into winners and losers. History doesn't recall if early homo sapiens gave a gold star to the child who speared the most small animals, but we can be sure there were cheers for the winner and laughter for losers. When a person fails, the emotional fall-out can turn inwards and/or outwards. If it turns inwards, feelings run towards inadequacy and self-doubt. If it turns outwards, feelings run towards envy, jealousy and resentment.

People who hold the strong, negative feelings of resentment often blame their lack of achievement on forces supposedly out of their control. They see themselves as victims – of class, colour, genetics, parenting, politics and whatever else couldn't possibly be their fault. It's an attitude that creates bitter laziness. Even worse, elements within society are ready, willing and eager to reinforce and exploit this resentment. Not making it? We understand it's not *your* fault. Vote for us and we'll straighten things out. The next thing you know, you've given away your personal power and nothing's changed. Which gives you something else to be bitter about.

The truth is, you're only a victim if you think you are. Born in the wrong class? So what? It makes things more difficult, but it doesn't make them impossible. Parents never loved you? So what? You can look back to what could have been and feel miserable, or look forward to what can be and find what you need. Take all the wasted energy of resentment and apply it towards achieving your goal, and you'll be happier *and* that much closer to what you want out of life. The only way to stop resentment is to stop worrying about the results of competition. Stop worrying about failure.

For those of us immersed in the consumer culture, it seems easier to stop breathing than give up traditional ideas of success. Ignore the car, house, salary, education, accent and the like, and what's left? Sure, you won't have uncomfortable feelings of resentment, but you'll probably be on the dole. The funny thing is, in my experience, people who are always measuring their success and failure achieve *less* than people who do their personal best and call it good. Die-hard competitors can never find the peace of mind true excellence demands. They're so worried about winning, they lose. People who compete with no one but themselves win because they don't *need* to.

The difference between 'need' and 'want' is the difference between resentment and peace of mind. It's also the difference between failure and success. Put it this way: you may *want* to own a Mercedes, but do you really *need* it? Maybe your life would be substantially better if you had a top-down Merc. Maybe your business partners would respect you more. Still, do you need the car? Will you feel somehow less of a person if you don't have one? If the answer is yes, you're going to put an awful lot of pressure on yourself. Every day you *don't* get closer to owning a Merc is one more day of anger and frustration. When you see someone swanning around in *your* car, is it any wonder you feel like ripping their lungs out?

I had a young client who worked for an ad agency. He turned to hypnosis as a relief from anxiety attacks. If his boss looked at him the wrong way or his ex-girlfriend asked him about work, his heart raced, he couldn't concentrate and he felt resentment towards everyone. He believed everyone else was doing better than he was. Since he only felt anxious when someone questioned his performance, I asked him to define success: twenty-two thousand pounds per year salary and an industry award. So if you're earning 21,999 pounds you're not a success? We haggled, until it became silly. What about those awards? Aren't they notoriously corrupt? By pinning his self-worth to factors beyond his control, in a business known for its ruthlessness, he was forever poised on a knife's edge. To rid himself of anxiety and resentment, he had to find a way to stop worrying about success . . . or failure.

The alternative is simply to lighten up. Relax. By all means, set whatever goals turn you on. There's nothing wrong with imagining gripping the wheel of a super-expensive sportscar, or admiring framed awards on the wall. People who want world peace are equally free to pursue their goals. Just don't stake your life on it. If you need something too much, you'll either fail from anxiety or make bad choices in the name of success. Our *real* needs are few: food, water, shelter and love. To stop resentment, think of anything else as strictly optional. It may be hell to drive an old banger or lose your job, but you'd survive. It may not be pleasant, but you won't die from the experience. You may even emerge a stronger person. In the final analysis, you may *want* to achieve, but you don't *need* to.

The more frantically you chase something, the further away it gets, and the more resentment you feel. If you try to get a drink of water from a stream by grabbing the water with both hands, you're left with nothing but angry fists. If you gently cup your hands and allow some water to spill out as you bring it to your mouth, you can drink deeply. This idea is illustrated by a Zen story . . .

A young man wanted to study swordsmanship with a Zen master.

He asked the master how long it would take to become an expert swordsman. The master looked at his potential student carefully and said, 'About six years.'

The young man shook his head sadly. 'My father is ill and needs me on the farm. I don't think I could study for six years. What if I study very hard?' The master considered this and said, 'If you study hard, ten years.'

'Ten years!' the young man said. 'I don't have ten years! What if I pay you for an intensive course?'

The master considered the idea. 'Hmm, an intensive course . . . Alright. Fifteen years.'

Beauty and the Beast

When fashion model Michelle Geddes was eighteen, she and two of her friends would hit the nightclub scene dressed to thrill. Men called the threesome 'the ice maidens' because they could 'freeze a man at twenty paces'. Obviously, a trio of young, drop-dead beautiful women flirting with every available man is not going to make other women feel comfortable. 'It was the first time I became aware of resentment,' Geddes remembers. 'Other women thought we were arrogant, because we supposedly knew we could have any man in the place. Even worse, they blamed us for making them feel bad about their own looks, showing them and everyone else their inadequacy. They'd stare at us with hate in their eyes, stand in our way, bump into us. These were not happy women.'

At the time, Geddes didn't pay much attention to the negative effect her looks could have on other women. Being beautiful was her job. If her physical appearance created ill-will in less conventionally attractive women, it was a small professional drawback. Four years and two children later, Geddes's understanding of envy and resentment has undergone a radical shift. 'Women are brought up to believe that looks are the key to getting what they want. To a degree they're right. It shouldn't be that way, but it is. Women make it worse for themselves by worshipping a very narrow idea of beauty. I make it worse. Young girls see me in something designed for someone slim and think they have to be a size ten to be sexy or successful. That kind of thinking creates terrible feelings of envy and resentment. Sometimes, it can even lead to anorexia.'

In the competitive world of professional modelling, there's plenty of opportunity for a model to experience resentment first-hand. Geddes experienced the feeling when she watched her friend Kate Moss's career take off. 'I was very protective of her before she became famous. I wanted her to do well. But now that she's hot, a part of me says it should have been me making loads and loads of money. I hear something about Kate and the instant response is envy, a wave of resentment. I can usually talk myself out of it by reassuring myself that it really is OK for others to do well. She deserves it.'

Although Geddes can keep things in perspective, she says some models are powered by envy. She sees the attitude as a disaster waiting to happen. 'Envious people don't like people very much, including themselves. They just can't feel that way constantly and be happy. It all goes horribly wrong when they try to tear down the thing they're going after. They end up tearing down themselves.' Geddes's hard-won insight into the emotion of resentment has led to a new sensitivity. 'I've changed since the days when I used to get dressed up to impress people. Now I go out like this [in jeans and an old sweatshirt]. I don't want people to look at me and feel envy. I want people to be happy with themselves, no matter what they look like.'

Confessions of a Pools Winner

Give Mona Skidmore credit for persistence. Every week for over fifteen years, this housewife filled in a ticket for the pools. She never expected to win, but playing the game was part of her life philosophy: 'If you don't put something out, you'll never get anything back.' On 6 June 1990, Mona got something back: £1,100,000. She remembers the afternoon after she'd reported her win: 'My husband and I had just finished lunch. We were sitting in the lounge having a cup of coffee. A big white car pulled up. A tubby man in a suit came to the door. There was an incredible stillness in the air. I remember thinking, that's it. Nothing's ever going to be the same again. Everything's going to change.'

And so it did. The Skidmores new-found fortune removed their financial worries and opened up a world of possibilities – from a cruise around the Canary Islands to buying drinks for their friends down at the pub. Mr Skidmore, a pensioner, stopped looking for free-lance teaching and engineering jobs. Their 33-year-old son Michael started chasing his lifelong dream of becoming a professional drummer. When they moved from their semi-detached house to a new house in a new neighbourhood, Mrs Skidmore realised that something else, something fundamental, had also changed.

'Before, when friends would come over to the house, you'd enjoy talking about the new things you bought. Everyone would share in your joy. Now, when I buy something, I can't talk about it . . . I see the sadness in their faces; it's not happiness like it used to be. I want to let them enjoy things with me, but they don't. It's lovely to share sometimes, but it seems as though you have to stop. I would love for all my friends to have the same as me.'

Mrs Skidmore enjoys her new lifestyle since the big win, but she senses 'a theme of sadness' running through her experience. One thing that makes her sad is the burning resentment she sometimes encounters. 'The people who resent our good luck are people who love money. I never knew how much some people love money; it's all they think about or talk about. I've learned that people who resent money live in a small world. They're boring people, and we don't have a lot to do with them. We buy them a drink and just laugh and think, how stupid can you be?'

Some might say it's easy to laugh at resentment when you're sitting on a cool million. Mrs Skidmore counters by saying that a person's attitude towards the good fortune of others boils down to a matter of belief: 'I believe when you really need a thing, it comes. If you have faith, it will come. It's all in the way you look at things.'

_ Plastic Surgery – The Kindest Cut of All? _

One thing that separates Mr Anthony Erian from other plastic surgeons is the large number of patients he turns away. The London surgeon specialises in face reconstruction and breast implants. The day before we spoke, he gently turned down twelve of twenty-two people who wanted him to change their appearance with his scalpel. On one hand, Mr Erian can afford to be picky; his services are in great demand. On the other hand, he can't afford *not* to be picky; dissatisfied customers can destroy a healthy practice. Over fourteen years, the doctor has learned how to identify and discourage patients who don't need or won't appreciate his skills. By and large, they are men and women suffering from resentment.

'Let's say a young woman works in a bank,' Mr Erian explains. 'She's single, looking for a relationship. Her best friend's getting all the dates. She's jealous. She can't hate her best friend, so she hates herself. She hates her image, her body, her face. She wants to get in touch with God about her deficiencies, but she can't. So she contacts a plastic surgeon instead. But I simply won't take on a patient if they've got too much anger or self-hatred. Surgery is not the answer to deep-seated psychological problems.'

Mr Erian appreciates the pressures which lead people to plastic surgery. 'The media's obsession with youth and health is one factor. Half of them say "I really want to have the face of Cindy Crawford". Another factor is increased mobility. When people stayed in one place all their lives, they were accepted by their neighbours no matter how they looked. When you move around, you're never quite sure of how people see you. But it's competition that really makes people resent their appearance. Society is far more competitive than it used to be. It creates a base line of what's acceptable, and some people can't achieve it. They feel hurt and angry. They say "How can I compete when I've got small boobs or bags under my eyes?"'

Some of these problems may strike you as perfectly reasonable. Mr Erian knows it's ultimately a judgement call, and there's always another surgeon ready to make the cut. The patients he accepts have come to terms with themselves *before* they walk in the door. They realise that everybody is good at something and have worked to cultivate that special part of themselves. They want to make themselves better, not perfect. As Mr Erian puts it: 'You can't be someone else. There's no surgery that will achieve that.'

Part Three

THE PROBLEM WITH PROBLEMS

'Nothing is more dangerous than an idea.
When it's the only one you have.'

Emile Chartier

9

Say Hello to Your Subconscious

Karen was a chocoholic. Every day, the 25-year-old accountant would emerge from the Tube, nip into the newsagent and buy four bars of milk chocolate. Every day, she'd tell herself she'd eat one bar and save the rest for later in the week. Every day, she'd sit down at her desk, work an hour, then eat all four chocolate bars. Then she'd feel guilty and sick. Karen really wanted to lose weight, feel more confident, buy sexier clothes. She knew her daily chocolate binge kept her from losing weight. She knew it was a bad habit, but she couldn't stop.

With regular hypnotherapy, Karen started to make changes in her eating habits. She began eating small amounts of healthy food throughout the day. She began exercising regularly. She learned to feel more relaxed about herself and her weight. But she still ate four chocolate bars every working day. For this reason Karen wasn't losing weight. Before the fourth session, Karen looked me in the eye and laid down the law, 'Either we sort this out or I'm going to stop hypnotherapy.'

I put Karen into a deep trance. I told her to forget the number four. Just like that: 'You will now forget the number four.' I asked her to count down from ten. She counted down to five, then stopped. Her face scrunched-up in frustration. She shifted around in the chair. She tried to recall the next number. After twenty seconds, Karen said 'three' and finished counting down. I told her she could now remember the number four and made sure she could count down from ten to one without any problems.

Then I said, 'From this moment on, you will forget the newsagent's shop outside your tube stop. When you reach the top of the stairs, you will simply think about something else. You won't even see the newsagent.' I wrapped the suggestion up with some positive thoughts about her new slimmer self. I inspired her with a vision of her future health, beauty and happiness. 'Because you won't bother with chocolate, you'll be able to look at your wardrobe and know you can fit into absolutely anything.' From the moment Karen came out of trance and opened her eyes, she thought the 'induced amnesia' idea was stupid.

'*Nothing* can make me forget about my milk chocolate bars,' she insisted.

The next session, Karen told me what had happened. 'I was walking up the stairs towards the street thinking how dumb your suggestion was. I was thinking, "This is stupid, it will never work." Then I forgot. It was weird. I walked past the newsagent without giving it a glance. I knew it was there, but I didn't really care. I went to work, sat down at my desk, did my work. I didn't even care about the chocolate.' These days, Karen has the occasional chocolate bar, but the four-bar habit is dead. She's lost a stone, her weight is stable and she looks fantastic.

Karen's success is available to everyone. It doesn't matter what your problem is: weight loss, smoking, anxiety, depression, poor body image, impotence, whatever. It doesn't matter how many diets you've tried, how many therapists you've seen, how much thinking you've done about your problem. It doesn't matter if you have less will-power than a two-year-old. All you need to do is learn a little theory about how your mind works and master a simple self-hypnosis technique. Once you've tapped into the power of your inner mind, you can create extraordinary effects. You can increase your memory, boost creativity, change habits forever and find health.

There are plenty of theories about how your mind works. Poets, priests, philosophers, psychologists and doctors all explore the mysteries of the human mind. The truth is, we're no closer to understanding how the human mind works than we were two thousand years ago. I believe there isn't a single answer, just lots of different ways of looking at the question. When it comes to theories or therapies, go with whatever works for you. For the purposes of this book, I'm keeping it simple. You don't have to know how an internal combustion engine works to improve your driving and you don't have to be a genius to change your life. The theory that unlocks the power of your mind starts with a simple concept: Your mind has two parts – the conscious and subconscious.

The conscious mind thinks, 'I wonder what's happening on that TV show I wanted to watch.' The conscious mind reasons, 'If I keep reading this book for another hour or so, I'll miss my programme.' The conscious mind weighs up alternatives, 'I really need to lose weight before the summer holidays, while my show will be on for the next decade.' It checks new ideas against past experience, 'Last time I read a self-help book I lost half a stone. Last time I watched TV I ate four-teen chocolate digestive biscuits.' The conscious mind guesses what might happen in the future. 'If I read a little faster, I'll still have time to turn on the television . . .' The conscious mind is the logical, rational part of your mind.

The conscious mind is also the least important part of your mind. Stop for a second and take that on board. The conscious mind is the least important part of your mind. Have you ever been told that we use only ten per cent of our brain? Rubbish. Do you use ten per cent of your heart? Do you use ten per cent of your eyes? Do you use ten per cent of your fingers? Why would nature give you a brain, and then hold ninety per cent of its power in reserve? For what? A rainy day? It's a bit silly, dividing up something as complex as your mind like it's an apple pie, but if we're playing the percentage game . . . *Ten per cent of your mind may be your conscious mind.*

Seeing your rational mind in perspective is not easy. Western society is based on the idea that conscious or rational thinking is the source of our personal power. We're taught to value rational thinking from an early age. Children are clever if they can figure things out – from their first picture puzzle to advanced algebra. Schools use stan-dardised tests to reward our ability to think clearly, without emotion or personal opinion. Financial analysts, dealers, computer program-mers, scientists, engineers, designers and other technical thinkers are the highly paid 'brains' of our times. Even entertainment appeals to our rational mind with complicated whodunnits and murder myster-ies. Supposedly, everything happens for a reason. If you don't know the reason, you're just not bright enough.

All this emphasis on the conscious mind leads to some bone-headed ideas. For one, we tend to think of our conscious mind as our 'self' – as if our ability to do the daily crossword is a measure of our true worth. For another, we begin to believe that people who get more out of life are more intelligent than we are. If only I was a little (or a lot) more intelligent I'd be happier. I'd find a way to lose weight, stop smoking, find a mate, get a better job, drive a nicer car, be less stressed, have stronger orgasms and discover a cure for cancer. Wrong. Granted, a conscious mind is a handy thing to have around – especially if you're trying to programme a VCR or pass your college exams. But it's not the key to personal growth and change.

If you could find health and happiness by rational thinking alone, you would have done it. You wouldn't be reading this book. You'd be doing what you want to do. You'd be the picture of perfect health. On a rational level, you know exactly what you need to change. You don't have to be Albert Einstein or Sigmund Freud to figure out what's wrong with you, what could be better or even why you're not healthy and happy. If conscious, rational thinking was the key to health and happiness, why are so many intelligent people so unhappy? In fact, you probably need to *stop* thinking about your problems so much. Look at it this way: the less conscious you are about all the reasons why you *can't* do something, the more likely it is that you'll keep trying until you *can* do it.

Many first-time clients talk about will-power. Forget will-power. Will-power is a myth. Change doesn't mean consciously forcing yourself to stop doing something you naturally want to do, or consciously forcing yourself to do something you naturally *don't* want to do. You can't change old habits by manipulating your rational mind any more than you can fly by flapping your arms. Rely on your rational mind for health and happiness and you're like the housewife wondering why the dishwasher is fading the colours on her fine china. As the dishwashing powder salesman says, 'The problem is *not* your dishwasher'. Your problems are *not* your conscious mind.

The key to change lies in the subconscious mind. That's the part of your mind that *doesn't* think. It reacts. How are you sitting right now? Feet up? Feet down? Did you decide to sit that way? Before you sat down did you say to yourself, 'Now, let's see. I'll sit down and place my legs at a forty-five-degree angle to my torso.' I doubt it. You probably sat down and made yourself comfortable, just like you always do. You didn't think about your sitting position any more than you decide how many times to blink to keep your eyes dust-free. Or how fast to breathe. Or when to get hungry. The subconscious mind controls the things you do but don't think about – sitting down, blinking, breathing, getting hungry and all the rest.

Psychologists call these non-thinking behaviours 'stimulus–response patterns'. To prove the existence of stimulus–response patterns, a Russian psychologist named Pavlov bought some dogs. Before feeding his dogs, Dr Pavlov rang a bell and measured the amount of saliva in their mouths. Then he fed them. Within a very short time the dogs salivated heavily right after the bell rang. Once the stimulus (bell) and response (salivate) pattern was set, Pavlov rang the bells at times other than feeding time. Every time he rang the bell the dogs salivated – regardless of whether or not food was on offer. Humans, Dr Pavlov insisted, are no less creatures of habit than dogs. Set a pattern, and it stays set in the subconscious mind.

Does this sound familiar? Let's say you're walking down the street and you smell pizza. You don't think you are hungry. You don't say, 'Hmmm, that smell indicates the presence of pizza, a baked dough food covered with a tomato-based sauce and various vegetables and meats. The last time I ate a pizza, I enjoyed the taste, texture and consistency. If I had a pizza now, I'd probably find it an equally satisfying experience. So I'll salivate in anticipation of the experience.' No. You smell, you salivate, you want to eat. Stimulus: pizza smell. Response: hunger!

Now imagine you're feeling really low. It's a week night, and all your friends are out. You think you should be doing something constructive like reading or laundry, but you can't be bothered. There's nothing on TV. No motivation, no company, no prospects. Do you know why you're feeling depressed? Do you know why the later it gets, the deeper you sink into your own personal rendition of the blues? Even if you do, does knowing the cause stop you feeling depressed? All of us are deeply influenced by our unthinking emotions: anger, fear, love, loneliness and more. Our emotions are often subconscious. They seem to be beyond our control. Some people automatically feel angry whenever they see a policeman. Stimulus: police. Response: anger. Others can't help feeling guilty at the very sound of their mother's voice. Stimulus: Mum. Response: guilt.

Perhaps there are certain times of day you always encounter your problem. Stressed executives are often their worst in the morning, while depressives dread the night. Maybe you find there are certain unpleasant situations you can't resist: confrontations with the boss, having sex with the wrong person or over-eating with friends. Maybe your aches and pains are terrible when you're bored, but completely forgotten when you're watching a film. Perhaps your memory for numbers stinks, but you can remember the lyrics of any fifties songs. All the things that you want to change about yourself can be seen as nothing more than habitual subconscious reactions to stimuli. Minus the fancy words, they are bad habits lodged deep in the subconscious mind.

Let's get something straight. You are not a 'bad' or 'weak' person because you haven't changed your bad habits. Strong subconscious urges are actually the sign of a powerful mind. Once you harness your subconscious energy, you can enjoy life a lot more than someone who can change his or her habits at the drop of a hat. A man who stops smoking one day simply because it makes the curtains smell is not likely to be highly imaginative or passionate. He probably never learned how to blow perfect smoke rings, or light a cigarette seductively. By the same token, he won't really enjoy *not* smoking. He'll never fully savour a lungful of fresh, clean air. If you're wrestling with strong habits, the chances are you have more *joie de vivre*, more 'life force' than even you suspect.

The subconscious is where this life force lives. It contains all your hopes, dreams and fantasies. When you sleep, you explore the kingdom of your subconscious, where anything and everything is possible. The subconscious is also the home of your imagination – your ability to create ideas and visions. And if that wasn't enough to tax anyone's brain, the subconscious is also a vast personal library where everything you've ever seen, heard, felt, smelled or tasted is stored. Whoever said we only use a small portion of our brain missed the point. The subconscious mind takes up the largest and most important part of our mind. It's constantly alert, active and aware. It's actually stronger than the conscious mind. This can be proven.

I had a client who was scared to death of flying. Marsha thought all this subconscious stuff was theoretical nonsense. In other words, her conscious mind didn't accept the power of her subconscious mind. I hypnotised Marsha and said, 'Your right arm is now as heavy as a lead weight. In fact, it's so heavy you can't lift it. It will remain heavy until I say it's back to normal.' I brought Marsha out of her trance. She couldn't lift her arm. 'Now Marsha,' I said. 'Are you completely awake and alert?' She was, but she couldn't lift her arm. 'There's nothing holding your arm down, is there?' Again she agreed, but couldn't lift her arm. 'You can't lift your arm because I said you can't while you were in a trance.' She accepted my reasoning, but couldn't move her arm.

There was no good reason why Marsha couldn't lift her arm. It wasn't damaged or restrained in any physical way. Her 'arm catalepsy' didn't make any logical sense. The only reason she couldn't lift her arm was because that's what her subconscious mind believed. No matter what Marsha thought consciously, no matter how silly or stupid my suggestion seemed, she couldn't lift her arm. When I told her subconscious that her arm was completely back to normal, so it was.

With experiments like this, I can convince the most sceptical clients that their conscious mind is weaker than their subconscious mind. Then, with a bit of hypnosis, I can usually erase or replace stimulus–response patterns. Marsha now feels a wave of calm the moment she steps on to an aeroplane.

Marsha didn't *have* to accept the supremacy of her subconscious mind for me to cure her fear of flying, just as you don't have to believe in the power of your subconscious to use self-hypnosis. The subconscious is there, working away, whether you like it or not. Of course, it's better to like it. If you come to hypnosis with an aggressive 'I'll show that subconscious who's boss' attitude, your chances of change are less than outstanding. If you approach your subconscious with a loving and accepting attitude, your chances of success are excellent. Your subconscious responds to love. Besides, your subconscious deserves your trust. It takes care of things like circulation, digestion, posture, blinking, respiration, muscle movement and speech – so you can get on with the business of living..

When it comes to working with your subconscious mind, it sometimes helps to think of it as a computer. The stimulus–response patterns or habits are like computer programmes. How did these programmes get there? From an early age, your subconscious mind was programmed by authority figures. First and foremost, there were your parents. From the moment you emerge from the womb, mummy and daddy are programming your subconscious mind. Food programmes are an example of how the process works.

Your subconscious need to eat, hunger, is switched on the moment the umbilical cord is cut. For many of us, the very first stimulus–response programme is crying equals food. Baby cries, mummy provides. Babies learn that making lots of noise with their lungs and throat leads to the nipple. They soon experiment with the programme to get it absolutely right. How much noise do I need to make to get food? Does it work every time? Then they learn that mummy is happy when they eat, and not so happy when baby re-decorates the kitchen walls with puréed carrots. As the baby grows up, when he is young and impressionable, his parents give his subconscious mind all sorts of food programmes:

food = reward	'Be good now and I'll give you some sweets.'
food = punishment	'Go straight to your room, young lady, and no supper for you!'
food = comfort	'That's all right, love, have some tea and a nice biscuit.'
food = family	'C'mon, let's all sit down to dinner now.'
food = celebration	'We're going to have birthday cake and ice cream!'
food = health	'Not feeling well? Have some chicken soup.'
food = excitement	'Let's all go some place new and have a big meal!'

Within a certain limit, subconscious programmes are healthy enough. There's nothing wrong with gathering your family around a table to enjoy good food and drink. If you're emotionally upset, a cup of tea and a biscuit sure beats a heroin injection. Of course, if you're trying to lose weight, a subconscious programme like 'comfort eating' is a problem. You discover that trying to fight this deeply rooted pattern is like arguing with your mother when you're twelve. The urge is more powerful than common sense. More powerful than your rational attempts to change it. Subconscious habits which can last a lifetime can be programmed into us in seconds.

I went to a horse show with my wife. I sat by the car on a picnic blanket, enjoying the warm summer sun. The family next to our horse box looked miserable: tense, sullen and always arguing with each other. They treated their horses like convicted criminals. The mother came back from her competition and asked her young son for the bottle of orange squash. He sheepishly admitted he'd finished the bottle. The mother grabbed her son roughly, looked him in the eye and yelled, 'You stupid, selfish boy!', as if the family was about to cross the Gobi desert and now everyone was going to die of thirst. Pavlov was nicer to his dogs, but the effect was the same. I could almost hear the subconscious programme clicking into place.

It's entirely possible that from that moment on the boy would equate finishing a bottle of drink with being 'bad'. His subconscious might have been programmed to think that he's basically a selfish moron. Maybe he was programmed to think sweet drinks are *really* important, because mummy got so mad.

Fortunately, most of us grew up in a healthier and more supportive environment. But all of us were programmed by our parents. Some programming is intentional, 'Always share your drink with others.' Some is unintentional, 'I'll whip that horse if he does that again.' Our young minds are like sponges, soaking up ways of reacting to the world and storing them in our subconscious mind.

Subconscious programmes are also implanted through personal experience, even when we're older. A client named Ken came to me for arachnophobia (fear of spiders). During our first session, Ken said he'd never been afraid of spiders until he stayed at a friend's cabin in the woods. Late one night, he went outside to the loo. He pulled the cord to turn on the light. There, not an inch from his face, dangled a spider the size of a small dog. (Well, it was tiny, really, but anything that close and unexpected in a strange and unfamiliar place looks like something from a science-fiction movie.) In that one instant, Ken's mind formed a subconscious programme linking spiders with danger, fear, panic, sweating, nausea, etc. Highly emotional experiences often have a tremendous subconscious effect.

At this point, it's vital to restate an important fact: You don't have to know why you have a subconscious programme to change it. It's interesting to know why you are afraid of spiders, but that knowledge is not necessary to change the habit. In fact, drop the word 'why' from your vocabulary. And here's where I lose almost all professional therapists. For most therapists, there is nothing more important than why you have a problem. That's their therapy. Understand why you like sweet drinks and you'll stop drinking them. Understand why you're afraid of spiders and you'll stop being afraid. Understand why you feel small at work and you'll hold your head a little higher. You'll 'come to terms with it'. You'll 'grow as a person'. Maybe. If understanding led to cure in even fifty per cent of cases, I'd be out of a job.

I had a client named Jennifer who was afraid of the colour red. If she saw anything bright red she felt extremely anxious. She started to sweat and couldn't concentrate. It was a strange but not particularly life-threatening problem. One day, she came into work and found that her new boss was a redhead. Jennifer went to psychotherapy for two years. At the end of her therapy she knew exactly why she was afraid of red. When she was about five, her mother held her hand over a red-hot electric hob to show her not to touch the stove. She had come to terms with her feelings with her mother. She had come to terms with her own weakness. But she was still afraid of red. Only through hypnosis was she able to completely alter her stimulus (red) – response (anxiety) pattern.

Hypnosis offers a fast, effective way to change your habits. You hypnotise yourself to gain access to your inner mind, command it to change, then inspire it with visions of future happiness. Forget past trauma and old, bad habits. What do you want to do when you achieve your goals? Buy new clothes? Feel more confident? You have to look forward to your goal, rather than backwards at your past. I can point to dozens of successful cases of men and women who have changed their lives in this way when all other methods have failed. Of course, hypnosis is not *the* answer, it's *an* answer.

More importantly, ask yourself how this idea feels. Does it make more sense to you to inspire yourself than to bash yourself on the head with painful past experiences and missed opportunities? If you were a subconscious mind, wouldn't you prefer to move ahead to success rather than contemplate past failure?

Remember Karen the chocoholic's disappearing number and forgotten newsagent? Once I had hypnotised her deeply, I had access to her subconscious mind. I could simply reprogramme her subconscious mind to forget the number four or her corner shop. As the authority figure, I could make changes in her inner mind and inspire her to lose weight. With self-hypnosis, you can become your own authority

figure. You reprogramme yourself. You inspire yourself. This kind of
subconscious reprogramming may or may not be as rapid as treatment from a professional therapist, but it puts you in the driver's seat.
It's a process that lets you take control of your own inner mind. Even
before you start that process, start thinking about your subconscious
mind – your inner self – in a new way.

Try this. Think of your subconscious mind as a five-year-old child.
The child believes in Santa Claus, fairies and goblins and mummy as
centre of the universe. Think of your current, negative eating patterns
as a teddy bear the child is clutching for comfort and security. It's an
old and ratty teddy. It's falling to bits. It's completely unsanitary. But
the child loves it. As an intelligent adult, you could trick the child,
wrench the teddy from the child's arms and be done with it. The child
wouldn't be too happy. In fact, the child would throw a tantrum, and
you'd probably end up giving back the teddy in order to keep your
own sanity. That's like trying to change your own bad habits by conscious 'will-power'.

Instead, you could win the child's confidence by saying, 'Old ted is
really lovely, isn't he?' Then you could smile warmly at the child and
show her a really lovely new teddy. 'Isn't this bear lovely, too? Maybe
ted would like to meet his new friend.' You could gradually lead the
child to play with the new teddy. With enough encouragement, the
child would soon leave old ted to the teddy bear retirement home for
some well-deserved rest. The child would have a new and better
companion. That's all the theory you need to practise HypnoHealth.
It's a technique based on kind, gentle and understanding authority.

In the next few days, begin the process of change by being kind to
your 'inner self' or subconscious mind. Treat yourself to a massage or
a walk through the park or – a new teddy. Now you have a new way
of looking at what's going on in your mind, forget about it. So you
inherited some duff subconscious programmes. No problem. All you
have to do is identify those subconscious thought or behaviour programmes, put yourself in a trance and slowly but surely change them
for good. The only reason you haven't found health and happiness is
because you didn't experiment with a few simple ideas. Relax, the
change has already begun.

10

What's Your Problem?

Choosing a Goal

When new clients come to the Farago Clinic they begin their therapy
by filling out a form. On a single sheet of paper they write their name,
address, phone number and a few details about any prescription drugs
they might be taking. Then clients are asked to state their goal. More
than a few people sit back in the leather chair and think a bit. Then
they ask, 'Can I make a list?' Others leave the form blank. They want
to tell me all their troubles, then have me choose a goal for them. Some
write vague or timid goals like 'I want to be a bit more happy'. Some
think too hard. They want to 'stop comfort eating' or 'establish a positive self-image independent of my husband's emotional blackmail'.
Establishing a simple and clear goal isn't easy, but it's vital to your
success.

The longest journey starts with a single step; the greatest hypnotherapy starts with a single goal. I've helped overweight smokers
also suffering from caffeine addiction, insomnia and mild anxiety
attacks. I couldn't do it all in one go. The clients have to decide what
they want to tackle first. We work to solve that problem, then move
on. Fortunately, clients don't have to return to square one each time.
Their initial success empowers them. When they see that the habits of
a lifetime don't have to *last* a lifetime, this sense of possibility and
accomplishment helps them to conquer the next problem. And the
next. And the next.

If you don't know what to change first, choose a problem that might
be relatively easy to shift. You probably have a good sense of which
habits are deeply rooted, and which habits are ripe for changing. At
the same time, set a goal that's dramatic enough to inspire you
onwards. You can use hypnosis to make yourself eat a high-fibre
breakfast cereal, but that won't inspire you much further than the toilet. Much better to kick a bad habit or start a good one. Decide what

would impress *you*. An overweight person who's been smoking for years may want to stop smoking first, to prove that they can conquer their longest-held, most destructive habit. Or they may prefer to lose a bit of weight, to bolster their overall self-confidence. It might depend on whether they're more motivated by health or appearance.

Avoid negative goals. It would be great not to have backache, but it's far better to have a relaxed, flexible back. Not having anxiety attacks is desirable, but not as desirable as feeling calm, confident and relaxed in every situation. If you become an ex-alcoholic, that will be a great relief to everyone around you, but not as great an achievement as becoming a loving part of your family. By choosing a positive goal, you're already inspiring your subconscious to change. It's equally important to set a goal you can measure. 'I want to feel better about myself' is a fine goal, but how will you know when you've succeeded? Better how? How much better? A more achievable goal would be, 'I want to feel better about myself when I'm around potential lovers.' Better still is 'I want a lover.' When you get one, you know you've reached your goal.

Don't go for broke. Set an achievable goal, so you can get into the habit of achieving. In the example above, you could start off with a goal of two dates a month and work your way up to Mr or Ms Right. For a bulimic, reducing the number of daily purges by one per week may seem a fairly minor goal. However, one day without bulimia makes the second and third day without the problem far more likely. Going 'cold turkey', stopping a habit entirely in one go, is a particularly bad idea. Cutting down on a habit gives you the confidence you need to stop it once and for all. Set a goal that you can achieve, and you'll be ready for the next challenge, and the next, and the next.

Choosing a goal shouldn't be stressful. Take it easy on yourself. Don't measure yourself against some perfect ideal. You'll be setting yourself up for failure. Good health is a trend, not a series of tick marks against a list of faults. Nor is happiness a question of identifying and curing the 'mother of all problems'. It really doesn't matter which goal you choose.

The following section examines the ten most common problems hypnotherapy clients bring to the Farago Clinic: smoking, weight loss, phobias, low self-esteem, insomnia, breast enhancement, stress, brain power and sex. The text offers practical, pre-hypnotic advice for people whose problems fall within these categories. It's *not* intended as a cure. The suggestions are designed to show you a gentle path from where you are to where you will be. As you read the section about your particular problem, try to see your situation from a fresh perspective. By seeing yourself and your goals in a new way, you prepare your inner mind for the seeds of change planted during self-hypnosis.

If your problem doesn't appear on this list, don't worry. While common sense advice is always helpful, the only hypnotic preparation you really need is a desire to change and a vision of a better life. Provided you have these two ingredients, you have everything you need to change your life with the power of self-hypnosis. Skip ahead to Part Four and begin.

There is one piece of advice which works for all of life's challenges: relax. If you can let go of your tensions and cares and worries and doubts, you clear the way for positive possibilities. Anything that relaxes you – a hot bath, massage, reading a good book, walking the dogs, playing with the kids, a nice cup of tea – helps you on your journey. Anything that makes you tired or stressed – people you don't like, working late, too much alcohol, arguments with your partner – blocks your progress. Seek out relaxation wherever you can find it. Why *not* relax? Anything's possible once you know how.

Giving up Smoking

More people go to a hypnotherapist to stop smoking than for any other problem. Any hypnotherapist who claims more than a fifty per cent success rate with these clients is either very good at hypnotherapy or very bad at statistics. It is not easy to stop smoking. Smoking is not a bad habit. Not entirely, anyway. I used to smoke, and I loved it. It was relaxing, excellent for concentration, a nice way to kill time, a good way to meet people and it made me feel cool. Unlike fear of spiders or over-eating, smoking generates positive feedback in a range of situations. In some ways, it's surprising anyone ever decides to stop. But that's exactly what you've got to do: *decide to stop*.

These days, smokers are surrounded by ex-smokers, employers and loved ones all desperate for them to kick the habit. Most of the time, the 'Quit Now' team beats smokers over the head with the health issue. You smoke, you die. (Or you smoke, I die.) Any honest smoker will admit that the thought of lung cancer is about as frightening as a car accident. It could happen and it would be ugly, but let's not think about it right now. Not while I'm driving. When I smoked, I never lit up a cigarette and thought, 'Uh oh, I'm one cigarette closer to lung cancer!' We do a lot of things that are dangerous or unhealthy over the long term, like driving fast or eating junk food. Why get fanatical? Death could come at any time. Lots of people with clean, pink lungs get run over by the proverbial bus. I say if you want to smoke, smoke and enjoy it.

If you're still with me, there's a good chance you actually want to quit. Even so, the decision to stop smoking has to be very strong for you to succeed. Smoking is a highly addictive habit. Hypnosis can't *make* you decide to quit the habit. It can only *help* you once you've made the decision. Let's get to it . . .

How well do you know your habit? Smoking is a stimulus–response pattern. You smoke in response to certain people, places or events. Thinking of yourself as 'a smoker' simply isn't good enough. Every smoker is different. Very few people smoke all the time. Some smoke in the car, some never smoke in the house, some smoke when they're stressed, some smoke to concentrate, some smoke in bursts of three, while others chainsmoke. If you want to stop all your smoking habits – because smoking is actually a collection of stimulus–response patterns – you need to know exactly when, where and why you smoke. You need to know all the psychological triggers that put a cigarette in your mouth.

Most smokers are not conscious of these triggers. How many times have you lit up without making a decision to smoke, or lit a cigarette when there was another one already going? To tackle the habit you need to become conscious of each cigarette. Make a list of every single cigarette you smoke from the time you wake up to the time you go to bed. If your habit changes significantly over the weekend, or when you go out for a meal, list all those variations as well. Note the time you smoke, the number of cigarettes you smoke, where you are, what you're doing and how you're feeling. For example:

TIME	NO.	WHERE	ACTIVITY	FEELINGS
8.00 a.m.	2	in the kitchen	reading the papers w/tea	hassled
8.30 a.m.	3	in the car	stuck in traffic	stressed, bored
9.00 a.m.	6	at my desk	calls, paperwork, coffee	active
12.00 p.m.	1	at a café	before sandwich	hungry
	1	at a café	after sandwich	full

Once you've listed every cigarette you can possibly remember, put a star next to those cigarettes which might be relatively easy to give up. When you start practising self-hypnosis, begin to stop smoking by eliminating these 'extra' cigarettes. For example, your initial goal could be to stop smoking at work, in the morning. A long-time, deeply rooted habit is not going to be cured in a day. Your list is simply a map from here (smoking) to there (non-smoking).

The next step is to get fed up. As I said before, there are lots of good reasons to smoke. In order to quit, you need even more powerful reasons to stop. Make a list of all things you don't like about smoking. Write down everything you can possibly think of: expense, smell, taste, breathlessness, threat of cancer, everything. Put your dislikes in order, from the absolute foulest thing about smoking right down to the smallest inconvenience.

You know cigarettes make your clothes smell, waste your money, reserve your place in the cancer ward and make you an addict. You're only halfway there. Don't make the mistake of thinking that a list of negatives equals a positive – giving up cigarettes. The only way you're going to get rid of this habit once and for all is to convince your subconscious that life without cigarettes will be better than life with cigarettes. You need a list of inspirational positives. Write down all the ways your life will be better without cigarettes. Don't use phrases like 'I won't smell of cigarettes' or 'I won't waste my money'. Make the entire list entirely positive: 'I *will* smell fresh and clean' and 'I *will* save money for my holidays'. The list of positives must be at least one idea longer than the list of negatives.

This list of positives is all the ammunition you need in your fight against your smoking habit. This is what will rid you of smoking. All you have to do is get this information deep down into your subconscious mind, where it can do you some good. You have to replace the smoking programmes with an even more powerful no-smoking programme. Self-hypnosis is the technique. Don't rush. You'll need time to get this right. A lot of smokers laugh and say, 'I'm good at quitting – I've done it loads of times!' Well, they're right. If you've quit before, you know what it's like not to smoke. You've had practice. You're just going to need *more* practice. If quitting was living hell, don't worry. You're starting from a fundamentally different place: the ocean of calm inside your mind.

At the same time, there's nothing wrong with using your conscious mind to reinforce your positive suggestions – as long as you do it in a loving, patient way. We get into habits like smoking through repetition. The more you smoke, the more you smoke, and the harder it is to stop. You can also use repetition to help get your positive suggestions deep into your mind. One simple method is to rewrite your inspirational list every morning when you get up and every evening before you go to bed. Why not place suggestions from the list in your home and work environment? For example, you could write, 'As a non-smoker, I save money for my holiday' on an index card and tape it next to an exotic postcard on your refrigerator. Or you could put a peel-off note saying, 'My children will breathe clean air' on a photograph of your kids in the office.

Another effective non-hypnotic suggestion is to work with 'symptom prescription'. In other words, take control of your habit by restricting or varying it slightly. It sounds strange, but changing your smoking habit in small ways (e.g. only smoke when you're standing up), gently takes your habit from subconscious to conscious control. Once smoking a cigarette becomes a more conscious decision, you have a far better chance of deciding to eliminate it. Change your smoking ritual. If there is a particular chair in your lounge where you always sit and smoke, move to another chair whenever you smoke. If you clean your ashtray after each cigarette, let it get completely filled up before emptying it. Or the other way around. Vary your routine as much as possible, so that the new routine is a nuisance and completely unpredictable.

Self-hypnosis will help your subconscious see that *not* smoking is desirable, but you can speed the process along by consciously making smoking undesirable. Remove as much of the pleasure as possible from the habit. Most smokers don't enjoy the actual act of smoking. They enjoy what they're doing when they smoke. So now, when you smoke, don't do anything else. Just smoke. No opening mail, no drinking coffee, no talking with friends, no driving the car, no glass of wine. No looking out of the window, thinking, planning, or dreaming. Just sit, staring at something really boring, and smoke. Smoke the cigarette all the way down in a really dull environment and you'll gradually realise just how unpleasant smoking really is. You'll be ready to hypnotise yourself to breathe fresh, clean air.

Staying Slim and Feeling Healthy

Weight loss is no big deal. Eat fewer calories than you use up and you lose weight. The pounds will drop away. Unfortunately, most people go about losing weight the wrong way: they diet. You don't need me to tell you that most diets don't work – or work for long. If you could lose weight and keep it off by dieting you wouldn't be reading this book. When it comes to dieting to lose weight, admit at least this much. You've been there and done that. It didn't work. Fortunately, losing weight doesn't have to mean reading diet books, counting calories, keeping charts, eating horrible foods and years of struggle. Losing weight can be a simple matter of changing your habits to create a healthy eating pattern. You don't have to diet, you have to *change* your diet. It's a subtle difference, but add a little self-hypnosis and it's the difference between success and failure.

Most diets don't work because they make you hungry. Hunger is one of our deepest subconscious urges. If you don't eat, you die, and your subconscious is having none of that. When your blood sugar reaches a certain low level – when there aren't enough calories in your bloodstream – your subconscious sends you a message to eat. The subconscious doesn't know how much fat you have stored up. It just knows you need food. Once you get this message, once you feel hungry, you can either eat or not. It's your choice – to a point. The longer you wait, the hungrier you get. Sooner or later you'll have to eat. If you let it go too long, you have no control and you over-eat.

At some point, your blood sugar reaches rock bottom, your subconscious takes control and you'll eat whether you want to or not. I treated an anorexic client named Annie who would starve herself for five or six days. Then, suddenly, she'd lose consciousness. She'd walk into a supermarket, open a food packet at random and eat the contents on the spot. Sometimes she awoke from this trance state in the shop, sometimes after she'd been accosted by the manager on the pavement. Annie's experience may sound extreme, but it's the logical extension of what has become a normal dieting pattern. Dieters are fighting a losing battle. They resist their subconscious hunger as long as they can, then over-eat. The truth is you can run, but you can't hide from your subconscious urges.

Diets are a binge-and-starve cycle. Some people go through it every single day of their lives. They over-eat at night (binge), then eat very little all day (starve). A very-low-calorie diet is often an extended-play record of the same tune. You under-eat for a couple of weeks, then revert to normal patterns of over-eating and the weight goes straight back on. When this pattern goes seriously haywire, it leads to anorexia and bulimia. The reason a person over-eats after under-eating is simple. They've trained their subconscious mind to believe that there's only one real opportunity to eat the food they need to survive. When that opportunity arrives, the subconscious is like a camel reaching an oasis. It takes in as much as it can, stocking up for the next trip across the desert.

This analysis doesn't seem to take into account emotional factors. Many clients report that they only over-eat when they're bored, depressed, lonely, etc. Anorexics and bulimics are often fascinated by the emotional reasons leading to their disorder. While psychology certainly triggers over-eating and eating disorders, I believe it's not as important as simple body chemistry. These psychological triggers come into force *after* you're hungry. Even in cases where emotions do play the crucial role, it's easier and more effective to set up a healthy eating pattern first, then tackle emotional problems. The truth is you don't need to know why you over-eat to control your eating. All you have to do is eat enough of the right foods so that you're not hungry. *Then* you can tackle the underlying emotional issues, if there are any.

Food is not your enemy. Hunger is your enemy.

It's a strange idea – eat to lose weight or avoid eating disorders – but it works. If you go into a supermarket when you're really hungry, what kinds of food do you buy? Most people buy junk food: microwave meals, crisps, biscuits, fizzy drinks – anything that doesn't require a lot of thought or preparation. When you're hungry, your shopping is in direct response to an urgent subconscious message: I need food *now*. This need for instant gratification leads you towards the chocolate, and away from the salads. On the other hand, if you do your food shopping when you've just had a meal, you will probably buy healthier foods. A fresh head of lettuce can compete with a brightly coloured chocolate-bar wrapper. You can even imagine taking the time to cook and prepare a proper meal.

Here's the new plan. Eat small amounts of healthy food throughout the day. (Do some research first if you need to learn what foods are healthy.) Steer towards fresh fruits and vegetables and lean meats. Cut down or eliminate full-fat dairy products like butter, milk, cheese and yoghurt. Reduce or eliminate your intake of caffeine (an appetite suppressant), so you can respond to hunger more successfully. Drink lots of mineral water. You don't have to give up fattening foods like chocolate entirely, just eat a whole lot less of them. That's it. Eat small amounts of healthy food throughout the day to keep hunger away. Then make sensible choices. That's what losing weight should be about: eating sensibly in a relaxed state of mind.

Eat breakfast. Something healthy like wholewheat toast with a butter substitute (if you can stand it), cereal with semi-skimmed or skimmed milk. Eat whatever you like that isn't too fattening, but don't get fanatical about it. Eat something healthy again mid-morning. A piece of fruit, carrots, low-fat yoghurt, raisins, whatever. Eat a good healthy lunch. A sandwich and soup, fruit, salad, something like that. Keep drinking lots of mineral water. Then eat again mid-afternoon. Another piece of fresh fruit or something else healthy. Have a healthy dinner with fresh vegetables and lean meats, fish or pasta, potatoes, rice, whatever you like that isn't pre-packaged, smothered in sauce or high in calories. If you feel hungry later, have a healthy snack.

Let me warn you straightaway: this method is not going to be fast. You'll lose between one and two pounds a week. But every pound off will be a pound off for good. And from the moment you start this new pattern, your energy levels will increase dramatically. You can use this energy to work-out, take a twenty-minute daily walk or try some other type of exercise. Then you'll lose even more weight, even more easily. Or simply feel healthier. Above all, you won't be dieting. You'll be eating sensibly, and losing weight.

So what does all this have to do with hypnosis? First, you can't hypnotise yourself to do something that runs counter to a natural, subconscious urge. You can't hypnotise yourself to stay on a rigid, hunger-producing diet. Hypnosis works best *with* your inner mind's survival instinct, not against it. The above weight-loss programme is the only one I know that combines well with self-hypnosis. Also, by keeping away hunger with an easy, sensible plan, you'll keep away food obsession. You'll feel satisfied, so you won't have to think about dieting or food all the time. Lastly, and perhaps most importantly, you need energy to change your subconscious. Energy requires food.

The hypnotic strategy is simple. To begin with, you need to know how much food you're eating and when you're eating it. Make a list of an entire day's eating, from the moment you wake up, to the moment you go to sleep. (Do not count calories!) Note the time, the food and drink, and whether it's healthy or unhealthy. Also note how hungry you are *before* you eat the food. For example:

TIME	ATE	HEALTHY?	HUNGRY?
7.30 a.m.	wholewheat toast with loads of butter 2 cups of tea, full-fat milk, sugar	not so healthy	not so hungry
10.45 a.m.	sticky bun from trolley 2 cups of coffee, milk	unhealthy	really hungry
1.30 p.m.	tuna, chicken sandwich bag of ready salted crisps 2 cups of tea	pretty healthy	starving

Next, make a list of all the things you hate about being over-weight or out of control: tight clothes, rude remarks, embarrassment in the changing room, money wasted on diet books, bad health, everything you can possibly think of. Then throw the list away. Too many people use their negative feelings towards their body to motivate themselves to lose weight or control their eating. It doesn't work. Being hard on yourself de-motivates your inner self completely. Now write this on a fresh piece of paper: 'I'm perfect now, but I'll be *more* perfect when I lose weight.' If it seems a lie, then lie. Soon enough it *will* be true. *That's* the belief you need to become slim and healthy.

Make a list of all the ways your life will be better once you've achieved your target weight: new clothes, energy, better job, good health, confidence on the beach, better sex, more self-respect, everything and anything. This list you keep. In fact, get it framed and hang it on the wall; put it on the fridge; photocopy it and leave it all around the house; recite it every morning and every night. Write individual suggestions on index cards and put them on every mirror in the house, and *especially* on the scales. Don't weigh yourself more than three times a week. The more you think about your own positive suggestions, the easier it will be to keep at it. Add the self-hypnosis, and you'll lose all the weight you need *and* improve your health easily, effortlessly and automatically.

Conquering a Phobia (Fear of Spiders, Aeroplanes, Enclosed Spaces, and More)

If you're afraid of something, don't be embarrassed. We're all afraid of something. An accountant who calmly Concordes back and forth across the Atlantic can be petrified of public speaking, while an airline pilot can go rigid at the thought of a tax audit. Fair enough, you may say; they're scared, but I've got a phobia. Phobia can be loosely defined as a severe fear reaction to a specific stimulus, such as a spider or aeroplane. Reactions can include hysteria, vomiting, panic and many other nasty involuntary symptoms. It's this involuntary aspect, this complete lack of control, that supposedly separates phobics from the 'merely' frightened. That may be true, but it's not important. Phobias are simply a logical if unpleasant extension of a natural fear response.

To cure your phobia, it's important to understand that you're not crazy or psychologically damaged. A phobia is a learned, subconscious response to a specific experience. Generally speaking, there's no need to unearth or explore the experience that created your phobia. For example, I used to be phobic of bees. Whenever I saw a bee, I ran. When I was in my late twenties, my mother told me about an early babysitter. This babysitter teased me mercilessly by saying, 'There's a bee on your head! There's a bee on your head!' until I panicked. I finally knew how and why I was phobic of bees, but I still ran. Only after I had a word with my subconscious mind could I become comfortable around bees. With a little persistence, a little courage and a lot of inner reassurance, you too can re-train your brain away from fear.

Before you set off on your journey to calm, you need a few good maps. First, you need to know *exactly* what makes you phobic. People who are afraid of flying are not all afraid of the same thing. Some are afraid of a terrorist bomb, some think the wings will fall off, others just don't accept the concept of flight. Arachnophobia (fear of spiders) can mean anything from fear of being bitten to fear of being crawled on, to fear of being caught in a web. Write down all the things that make you scared. Don't worry if they're rational or irrational fears. Then write down all your physical symptoms, in the order that they occur. Don't forget heartbeat, breathing, shivering or sweating, loose bowels, nervous twitches, shakes, etc.

Next, create a 'worst case' scenario. Start with the trigger, usually the thing that scares you. What is the worst thing that could happen? What's the worst thing that could happen next? And so on, right down to the absolute worst possible outcome. For example:

see a spider > spider scurries up to me > spider crawls on my leg > I can't move > I stop breathing > I start to suffocate > the spider bites me > I'm in pain as I suffocate to death

get into a lift > feel terrible > feel trapped > lift stops > can't breathe > can't move > people think I'm crazy > I go crazy > start crying > lift cable snaps > plunge to my death

The worst case scenario is a way to confront your fears. While self-hypnosis is perfect for easing your mind, there's no getting around the fact that you must eventually confront the thing that scares you. One of the most important psychological weapons you'll need for this showdown is knowledge. If you're afraid of lifts, find out their safety records. If spiders make you phobic, read all about their habits. Find out how planes fly, or what anti-terrorist measures airports are taking. Ask a lecture bureau how many people freeze on stage, or what makes a really good or bad public speaker. Do your homework. Read books, call experts, talk to friends. Become an expert in whatever makes you phobic.

The other weapon you'll need is positive encouragement. Make a list of all the ways your life will be better when you conquer your fear: increased self-confidence, getting to the top of tall buildings quickly, taking holidays in the country, going out more, flying to exotic places on holiday, etc. Make it a good long list, and review it often.

Once you've started practising self-hypnosis, you'll need a plan for 'de-sensitisation' therapy. That does *not* mean subjecting yourself to the full force of your fear again and again. The goal is slowly and gradually to expose yourself to more and more of your negative stimulus, until you feel more and more comfortable with it. An agoraphobic (fear of open spaces) should start with a short walk to the end of the pavement and back. Next, he or she can try to cross the street. And so on, until the fear is at least under control, at best cured. Arachnophobics can start with pictures of spiders, then look at an empty web, then look at a spider. People who are afraid of flying should do a bit of plane-spotting, then try a 'dry run' to the airport with packed bags, then a short flight.

Above all, give yourself time. There's no need to rush. You will overcome your fears eventually. At the same time, the lessons you learn about conquering fear will also apply to all the minor fears you experience when you try something new. Learn to take everything in your stride, and you can try more new things and grow more rapidly. I once did a fire-walking course where the organiser said, 'If you can walk on hot coals, you can ask your boss for a rise.'

If you can conquer your worst fear, there's no telling what you can do.

Building Confidence and Self-Esteem

When you lack confidence, life is an endless series of bungled opportunities. As soon as you come across a chance to achieve, you immediately suspect you're missing the vital something you need to succeed. You may not even try. If you do try and fail, it confirms your low opinion of your abilities. Then your self-doubts grow worse, and you're more reluctant to try again. If you try and succeed, you still can't quite shake the feeling that somehow you don't deserve your success. You feel uptight and defensive, waiting for someone to discover 'the truth' about you. Low self-esteem is a vicious circle of self-doubt and withdrawal. The less confidence you have, the harder it is to achieve. The harder it is to achieve, the less confidence you have. You *know* you need confidence to get out of the cycle, but confidence in what? Confidence in yourself.

It's extraordinary how we toss around the word 'self': myself, yourself, ourselves. The expression is so common that we've welded the two words into an inseparable whole. Yet only philosophers and poets take the time to stop and think about what this 'self' is all about. We know that our health and happiness depends on 'confidence in myself', but to what 'self' are we referring? The emotional, physical, financial, moral or spiritual self? The self that plays tennis, or the self that smiles when a baby smiles? The self that feels frightened, or the self that wants to have a go? For confidence, you need to tap into the power of your *inner* self. That's the self that's deeper than your rational thoughts, behaviour or emotions. Call it your subconscious mind, your soul, your inner child, whatever. If you want to feel calm, confident and relaxed in every situation, the answer lies within.

Of course it does. Anyone who ties their self-worth to external reality is setting themselves up for disappointment. It's a harsh world out there. Most people don't care about your self-esteem. With certain notable exceptions (your parents and friends perhaps) people are far too busy with their own lives to boost your confidence. Their opinions are also quite undependable. Whether they're complimenting you or insulting you, who knows if they're telling the truth?

The only confidence you can depend on is confidence in your inner self. Confidence in the power of your own thoughts. What you tell yourself – your thoughts – has the greatest impact on your entire life. Your thoughts have more influence on your health and happiness than your income, status, health, sex, weight, wit, intelligence, strength, character, everything. Your thoughts determine your emotional state. If you think negative and self-critical thoughts, you feel depressed and unhappy. If you're depressed and unhappy, you can't achieve. By the same token, if you think positive, self-flattering thoughts, you feel good. If you feel good, you can accomplish miracles. Your thoughts are the root source of all your personal power.

The key to confidence is to change the way you think about yourself. It helps to think of your future confident self as a beautiful building, strong enough to withstand any storm. How do you build a structure like that? Brick by brick. How do you build yourself into a confident person? Brick by brick. The bricks of your confidence are positive thoughts about yourself. Your parents, friends and teachers didn't give you enough encouragement and support to help you see yourself as a powerful, capable person. They didn't build you strong enough. So be it. Now you've got a second chance. Now you can build yourself according to *your* needs. Never forget that all your experiences – whether they were good or bad – have created a firm foundation for you to build on.

Most people encounter a re-construction problem; their standards are too high. They wait for massive accomplishments before they'll give themselves even a tiny pat on the back. That won't do. Bricks are small, and there are a lot of them. To build confidence, you have to give yourself a pat on the back for anything and everything. If you make a nice cup of tea, tell yourself, 'I made a nice cup of tea. Quite clever, really.' When you brush your teeth, tell yourself, 'Not bad, I brushed every single one.' If someone asks you the time, tell them, and while you're at it tell yourself, 'I handled that very well.' How far should you lower your standards? Lower them to the precise level that you're at right now. Right now, you can't afford to set your standards any higher than your accomplishments. You can't afford to see yourself as a failure.

Make a list of all the things you're good at. Make it a *long* list. Then, buy a small notebook to carry around with you. Every day, write down all the things you did well that day. Start with a minimum of ten, work your way up to twenty, then thirty and beyond. Read your list every morning and every evening. Get in the habit of complimenting other people; it helps you to see the good in yourself. Work to improve the things you do well, and give yourself credit for the things you don't do well. (After all, we can't all be good at everything.) Start setting achievable goals to help you feel more satisfied with your abilities. Once again, keep it very simple and easy, like making a better slice of toast or answering the phone well. Build your self-confidence gradually, brick by brick.

Above all, relax. Confidence is a state of mind – not a fancy car, a high salary or a red rosette. Practise your daily self-hypnosis to discover the ocean of calm and peace inside your subconscious. Use this technique to get in touch with yourself. You'll like what you find. In fact, when you really appreciate your 'self', you'll feel calm, confident and relaxed in every situation.

Curing Insomnia

Charlie couldn't get to sleep. More precisely, the semi-retired racing-car driver couldn't stay asleep. Every night, he'd wake up after about five hours and couldn't get back to sleep. When Charlie came for hypnotherapy, I started with the usual battery of questions. Diet? One meal a day, red meat and potatoes, no vegetables. Tea or coffee? Yes please! Drink? A bottle of red wine every night. Work? About fourteen hours a day, seven days a week, no holidays for the last six years. Relaxation? Work is my relaxation. Worries? Loads. Sex life? Not really. Goal? Charlie wanted me to command his inner mind to sleep eight hours a night. I told him I couldn't do it. He'd have to change his lifestyle as well. Charlie opted out.

Insomnia is best cured by combining a number of solutions rather than a single 'quick fix'. While self-hypnosis is an entirely healthy and natural sleep aid, it works best in conjunction with a multi-pronged attack. Before the self-hypnosis technique can be truly effective you need to remove the barriers to sleep. What are those barriers? You know you need a certain number of hours of deep, refreshing sleep to stay healthy and happy, but do you know all the things that can keep you awake? Charlie's case history is a perfect example of an unintentional sleep-deprivation programme. When I pointed out some of the changes he needed to make Charlie ran a mile. If you're serious about sleep, you'll have to take a close look at your lifestyle.

A healthy diet is critical to restful sleep. Consult a good book, healthfood shop or dietitian to discover what foods and beverages keep you awake, and which help you to sleep. Above all, avoid stimulants like nicotine (cigarettes), caffeine and sugar. Most insomniacs keep away from tea and coffee but few are aware that many foods also contain caffeine (especially chocolate). Fewer still realise just how long caffeine and sugar stay in the bloodstream. You can still be on a caffeine high or sugar buzz four or five hours after your last coffee, tea, cola, chocolate bar, etc. The older you get, the longer it takes to process caffeine and sugar. While experimenting with your body chemistry, remember that drinking a cup of herbal tea or taking a natural sleep remedy before bed won't counteract an entire day's eating and drinking.

I'm not a vegetarian, but there's a great deal of evidence that people suffering from sleep problems should avoid red meat before bed. Meats like beef and lamb require far more time and energy to digest than other forms of protein. Eat a hearty steak, and your digestive system will be hard at work long into the night. In fact, it can take *days* for red meat to pass completely through your body. If your digestion system is constantly chugging away, it may be keeping the rest of your body awake. It's certainly worth trying a meatless week, or eating your meat at lunch rather than dinner. At the very least, eat the highest-quality meat possible. Seek out more easily-digested, organic meat.

Alcohol is another barrier to sleep. Many people turn to alcohol to ease them into oblivion. Oblivion is right, because alcohol-induced sleep is nothing like natural, deep sleep. You're sleeping drunk. Drunk sleep may be better than no sleep, but only just. Drink a bottle of red wine before bed and you dehydrate in your sleep. Even worse, the impurities in spirits severely tax your liver. Why put an enormous physical strain on your body at precisely the moment when it needs to rest and recuperate? Alcohol also releases inhibitions. Even if you're exhausted, these new thoughts and emotions can keep you switched on for hours. In short, alcohol disturbs your natural physical and mental energy patterns. Restrict it to lunchtime, or eliminate it altogether.

Most people work to live, but if you live to work you may not sleep. That could mean you lie in bed worrying about your work. Or it could mean you simply don't know how to relax. Relaxation is a skill. People who work too much usually lose the skill of relaxation. They don't take the time or make the effort to relax. They don't play sport, read books, go for long walks in the country, have a sauna, enjoy a massage or simply look around the office and say, 'Right then, I'm off.' When you lose the ability to relax, the mind is like a light switch. It has only two states of consciousness: awake and asleep. It's no surprise that people who work too much can't 'switch off.'

When you go to sleep, you're moving from consciousness to subconsciousness. Although people believe they're either asleep or awake, there are many states of consciousness between wakefulness and sleep (including trance). At least there *should* be. Some insomniacs have to retrain their mind to achieve these less-than-fully-awake but-not-totally-asleep mental states. They must gradually learn to ease their way down through the various stages of relaxation into sleep. It's really not that complicated. All they need do is learn to relax when they're awake. Then they can re-create the feeling when they want to sleep. There's a whole world of relaxation experiences available for conscious exploration: meditation, fishing, golf, books, exercise, sauna and, of course, self-hypnosis. Insomniacs who work too much have to work a lot less and relax a lot more.

And then there's worry. Worry is the number-one cause of sleeplessness. Right now, somewhere in the world, someone is lying in a bed, trying to sleep while imagining some awful disaster. It's a bit like trying to swim with lead weights tied to your ankles. Worry – projecting negatively into the future – sends a clear message to your inner mind: *danger!* The last thing your inner mind wants to do in a dangerous situation is go to sleep, even if the danger isn't 'real'. Only when the inner mind is thoroughly exhausted does it finally let down its guard and allow you to go to sleep. By that time, the alarm clock may be ready to go off.

There are many ways to stop worrying. Now may be a good time to read or re-read Chapter Six. One anti-worrying strategy not mentioned in that chapter is 'worry time'. Sometime in your day – *not at night* – set aside at least half an hour to have a good worry. Sit down somewhere quiet and worry. No phone calls. No interruptions. Just worry. Use a pad of paper if you like. Then, when it's time to sleep, tell yourself that you've done your worrying for the day. And you have! So you'll need something else to think about. Use the self-hypnosis technique, go to your special place and think about that. Or think about some happy memory. Or think about something really pleasant that may happen in the future. If you're still worrying uncontrollably, don't despair. Seek out some professional therapy.

What about sex? The need to procreate is one of our most basic instincts, buried deep in the subconscious mind. Although it is possible to live, love and sleep happily without any sex whatsoever, orgasmic release is vital to health and happiness. When a person ignores or neglects this need, the build-up of physical, mental, emotional and spiritual tension can prevent him or her from getting a proper night's sleep. A good sex life allows the release of tension deep sleep requires. People with a regular, healthy sex life suffer less from insomnia than people who sleep alone. Whether or not sex helps you sleep, increasing the frequency, intensity and creativity of your sex life will help increase your overall relaxation.

If you can clear away some or all of these barriers, self-hypnosis will be extremely effective. Although hypnosis is not sleep, it's closer to sleep than full consciousness. If offers insomniacs a bridge to the land of dreams. Even if you don't get to sleep, you'll get far more rest in a hypnotic trance than you will tossing and turning for hours trying to get to sleep.

Breast Enhancement

I'm amazed at how many people refuse to believe that hypnosis can make a woman's breasts larger. Tell someone that hypnosis can eliminate a smoking habit, no problem. Tell them hypnosis can cure a phobia or depression, no problem. Tell them hypnosis can numb a part of the body so much that a person can have an operation without anaesthesia, and they can just about handle the concept. Tell them that hypnosis can make a woman's breasts larger, and they think you're either barking mad or a quack. They accept the power of the inner mind to change life-long habits, heal psychological wounds and alter physical sensations, but they can't accept the idea that hypnosis can change a woman's body shape.

Hypnotic breast enhancement makes perfect sense. First of all, we're not talking about adding height, altering ear shapes or messing about with body parts that generally grow, form and stop growing. *Women's breasts change size all the time.* A woman's breasts grow immediately before her period, by as much as half an inch. They grow when she puts on weight. They swell by as much as thirty-five per cent when she's having sex. They grow a great deal when she's pregnant. Her breasts can grow even when she *thinks* she's pregnant. Hypnotic breast enhancement is simply a matter of tapping into the natural growth process and taking control. Once you have control, you simply command the body to create the growth.

The first theory on how hypnotic breast enhancement works starts with the subconscious. The subconscious controls your autonomic body functions: heart rate, blood flow, breathing, digestive juices, hormones, etc. On a cold day, your subconscious automatically directs the blood away from your fingers and toes, to protect your internal organs. The same thing happens when you watch a horror movie. During sex, the subconscious sends blood rushing outwards; a woman's breasts and a man's penis swell in response to sexual stimulus. Normally, you don't consciously change your blood flow, but you *can*. Stick your head in a refrigerator. Watch a scary movie. Masturbate, or have sex. In all three cases, you will alter your blood flow by a conscious decision. You will alter your body chemistry by your behaviour.

You can also alter body chemistry by thought. If you think about an axe murderer lurking somewhere in your house or flat, really imagine the axe swishing through the air high above your head, your fear will change your heart rate, blood flow and adrenalin secretion. It's the same concept when someone says 'think warm thoughts' on a cold day. They're essentially telling you to trick your subconscious into believing that it's warm, so that the subconscious will send warm blood out to your extremities. That's hypnotic breast-enhancement theory number one. You enter a deep trance, think warm thoughts and direct the subconscious to send blood rushing into your breasts. Do that often enough, and the breasts will swell and grow to accommodate the extra blood supply.

Breast-enhancement theory number two involves the endocrine system. The endocrine gland is the part of your body that secretes the hormones responsible for your sexual cycles and (to an extent) behaviour: oestrogen, androgen, testosterone and others. A woman in trance can send her subconscious mind a message to grow her breasts through visualisation (imagining larger breasts) and direct suggestion (commanding her body to change). The subconscious then stimulates the endocrine gland to release natural growth hormones. These hormones make the breasts grow larger. To take advantage of this hypnotically, a woman can recall the physical sensations felt during puberty, pregnancy and breastfeeding (if experienced). She 'tricks' the subconscious into releasing the growth hormone.

It doesn't really matter which theory you believe, if any. The important point is that hypnotic breast enhancement is a scientific fact. In 1949, a practitioner used hypnosis to enhance the breasts of twenty women aged twenty to thirty-five. Seventeen out of twenty subjects increased their breast size by about one to one-and-a-half inches. Five women achieved growth of about two inches.* In 1974, thirteen women in another experiment increased their breasts by an average of 2.11 inches.† In 1977, twenty-two American university students and staff achieved an average increase of 1.37 inches.‡ All these results were independent of weight gain or menstrual cycles.

Unlike surgery, hypnotic breast enhancement can't create instant results. At best it's a slow process. At the Farago Clinic, the average increase in breast size is about half an inch per eight one-hour sessions (in addition to daily self-hypnosis). That's *after* I've turned away clients who are unrealistic, non-hypnotic or unmotivated. You'll need two things to succeed with self-hypnotic breast enhancement: belief and patience. Belief is both the petrol and the engine of hypnosis. The inner part of your mind must accept that something is possible before it will try to achieve it. Patience is simply your willingness to go the distance. If you don't believe hypnotic breast enhancement is possible, don't bother. If you aren't willing to practise self-hypnosis every day for a minimum of two months, don't even start.

For those women who want to give hypnotic breast enhancement a chance, there's another important consideration. Many women who try this therapy have a very poor body image. They hate the way their breasts look, and they're generally uncomfortable with their own sexuality. More than a few have been sexually abused. The single largest block to success is self-loathing. You simply cannot convince your inner mind to make your breasts grow if you hate your body. Self-hatred is a very clear and powerful subconscious message. It says 'Why bother? You'll always look horrible.' You have to remove those negative thoughts *before* you start. Work on your self-confidence first. Then look at a *Playboy* centrefold. If the image makes you burn with envy, work on eliminating those feelings. If you can use the image to inspire yourself, you're ready.

Overcoming Stress

We're all suffering from stress. Life today is so much faster and more complicated than it used to be. Modern living creates stress. It causes

* L.M. Lecron, 'Breast Development through Hypnotic Suggestion', *Journal of the American Society of Psychosomatic Dentistry and Medicine*, 16, 1969, pp. 58–61.
† J.E. Williams, 'Stimulation of Breast Growth by Hypnosis', *Journal of Sex Research*, 10 (4), 1974, pp. 316–26.
‡ Allan R. Staib and D.R. Logan, 'Hypnotic Stimulation of Breast Growth', *American Journal of Clinical Hypnosis*, Vol. 19, No. 4, April 1977, pp. 201–8.

heart attacks and ulcers, ruins relationships and leads us into despair
and misery. Of course, we need a certain amount of stress to fight the
battles of life. So there's good and bad stress. Good stress keeps us alive;
bad stress kills us (at least in the long run). To really get a grip on this
deadly disease, you have to learn from an expert in stress management.

Rubbish. The concept of stress as a modern-day affliction requiring
specialist attention is a myth. First of all, we're not all suffering from
stress. There are plenty of people who take life calmly, who don't get
unduly upset when things don't go their way. You'll find a lot more of
them tanning in Hawaii than driving in Paris, but you can find relaxed
people all over the world. Second, life is no more pressurised than it
was two hundred or two thousand years ago. Fighting a battle for
your life or hunting for your next meal is at least as stressful as fighting for a parking place. Third, stress doesn't necessarily lead to heart
attacks and despair. You don't have to go any further than a bond
dealer's room to see people thriving on pressure and aggravation.
Lastly, you are the only stress expert you need.

Start with a proper definition of stress. Stress is an what we feel
when we're unable to counter or accommodate negative thoughts,
people or events – when we can't feel calm, confident and relaxed in
the face of perceived danger. Given this definition, it's easy to see how
slippery the word stress can be. How can you say stress is any one
thing to any one person? For example, polar explorer Robert Swan is
so stressed by traffic jams that he only drives a motorcycle. He
couldn't imagine sitting in an enclosed box, waiting for someone else
to do something. On the other hand, I had a client who did his best
thinking in traffic jams. He actually looked forward to them! One
man's stress is another man's cherished thinking time.

To beat stress, you have to know *exactly* what makes you stressed.
Stress is a very specific, very personal stimulus–response programme.
It's no good simply saying, 'I get stressed at work.' When do you get
stressed at work? Exactly what makes you feel tense or nervous? If the
boss is making your blood boil, what is it about him that sets you off?
Something he says? Something he does? Something he is? 'My husband gets me stressed' is another typically vague analysis. He probably doesn't get you stressed when he's sleeping, so when *does* he wind
you up? What does he say or do? Right now, take a sheet of paper
and describe your stress creator in as much detail as possible. List
what, when, where, who and how, in whatever order works best. For
example:

WHO: boss WHEN: whenever he's in a bad mood, about 3 times a week, usually
Monday or Tuesday and definitely Friday WHERE: in my office, by the coffee-

maker, in his office WHAT: he thinks I'm not working hard enough to get the business, doesn't like me, never did HOW: he yells at me, accuses me, threatens me, humiliates me in front of secretaries, makes me apologise for things that aren't my fault

Next, the other side of the equation: your reaction. Stress often triggers dramatic physiological changes – what researchers call the 'fight or flight' syndrome. In other words, your subconscious prepares your body for confrontation (fight) or retreat (flight). Depending on your personal chemistry and the severity of the perceived danger, your heartrate soars, the blood flows inwards (to protect your internal organs), adrenalin courses through your bloodstream and your body's systems go on red alert. Great stuff if you're fighting hand-to-hand combat or running away from a lion. Not so terrific if you're stuck in a traffic jam, changing nappies or dealing with the phone company.

To take control of your stress reactions, first note your physical symptoms. How do you experience stress in your body? Do you feel dizziness, heartburn, excessive perspiration, nausea? Then write down your emotional reactions, such as anxiety or depression. What is the sequence of events? Does the stress build slowly or hit you like a freight train?

On a separate piece of paper, write down your stress stimulus. Then list all your reactions to your negative stimuli. Describe the physical and emotional symptoms, the sequence of events, how long the symptoms last and how you try to cope. For example:

SHOW-DOWN WITH THE BOSS

PHYSICAL SYMPTOMS: sweaty palms, funny tummy, collar gets too tight, hop from foot to foot when he's talking, inability to speak coherently EMOTIONAL SYMPTOMS: anxious, worried, defensive, hurt, angry, embarrassed, guilty, angry again, depressed SEQUENCE OF EVENTS: tension starts slowly as soon as I see him, gets worse and worse as he starts yelling, full reaction within two minutes HOW LONG THE SYMPTOMS LAST: all day HOW I TRY TO COPE: keep my mouth shut while he's talking, drive home swearing, have two large Scotches, watch TV, sleep

The easiest way to 'cure' stress is to avoid whatever it is that gets you stressed. Self-hypnosis can reprogramme your reactions to negative stimuli, but the fastest solution is not to get stressed in the first place. In the example above, the client knows roughly when the boss is on the rampage. The stressed employee could leave the office or make an important phone call to avoid and delay the stress-creator. Cowardly or sensible? Eventually, the boss would learn either to cool down or find someone else to persecute. In the same way, Robert Swan cured his stuck-in-traffic stress by gliding through jams on his motor-cycle. Someone less brave could vary his or her commuting time to miss the worst of the traffic. When it comes to relieving stress, a little avoidance can go a long way.

I treated an advertising copywriter named Kenny, who was con-stantly stressed at work. Quite clearly, Kenny didn't enjoy the cut-throat world of advertising. At the first session, I suggested he find a writing job in a more laidback industry. That idea didn't figure in his list of options, so we worked on eliminating Kenny's negative stimu-lus–response patterns. He was fired before our fourth session. At that point, Kenny was unemployed but cured. He no longer needed ther-apy. Common sense says sometimes it's best to steer clear of the things you don't like.

If you can't avoid the stressful person or event, you need to change the way you think. If the boss jumps down your throat, say to your-self, 'My boss criticises me because *he's* uptight. But I'm not going to make his problem my problem.' With a little practice, you can use rational thinking to change your thoughts and calm yourself before, during or after stressful people or events. For example, stand in a bank queue thinking about the lazy and inefficient staff and you'll feel stressed. Think instead about that lovely holiday you'll be spending in the sun and you won't even notice the queue. Your thoughts are the link between the stimulus (bank queue) and the response (stress). Change your thoughts and you break the link.

This re-thinking process is sometimes called 'cognitive therapy'. Cognitive therapy works best if you practise it often, and experiment with both the strength and duration of your stress reactions. For example, in a traffic jam, give yourself a finite amount of time to be stressed. Tell yourself that you'll be well and truly stressed for five minutes. Then turn on the radio and think about every word of the news. Then, after the news, decide whether or not you want to be stressed. You can learn literally to schedule your stress. Once you've taken control, you can vent your stress reactions at a safe place and time. Exercise is a tremendous stress release as is self-hypnosis.

Sometimes it's impossible to think rationally. You can *try* to reason with yourself. You can tell yourself to stay calm when your husband's late, or the traffic grinds to a halt but it's hard not to grow more and more aggravated as the minutes tick by. The subconscious stimulus (husband late, bad traffic) – response (aggravation) pattern may be too strong to defeat by conscious thought alone. In these cases, self-hypno-sis is the answer. It can break the stimulus–response pattern by implanting a new thought pattern deep in your mind. One of the rules of the inner mind is, 'What can be conceived can be created'. Imagine yourself living in a relaxed stress-free world, and you will have taken the first step to creating it.

Improving Brain Power

Albert Einstein had a problem. He wanted to know more about the nature of light. So the physicist decided to row out to the middle of Lake Geneva and have a think. Bobbing about in his rented boat, Einstein looked up into the star-filled sky. He imagined himself riding a beam of light into the inky blackness of space. He imagined himself passing a planet. He felt gravity sucking him towards the planet. 'That's it!' he thought. 'Light bends!' His mind raced with the implications. He grabbed the oars and . . . what? He'd forgotten how to row! The father of modern physics couldn't remember which way to face and how to move the oars. When he finally returned to the boatyard, did the boatman say, 'Einstein, boy, what a genius!' Probably not.

Chances are you're neither a genius nor a moron. Most humans fall within a limited range of basic intelligence. You may not be a Nobel-prize winning mathematician, but you and billions like you can cook a meal or row a boat. It's easy to be over-awed by highly educated professionals and successful people. It's easy to believe that your status in life is somehow related to your mental ability. Don't you believe it. Never forget that almost all education systems reward conformity rather than intelligence or creativity. Put aside personal issues of success and failure, and you can begin to see the truth about mental ability. If someone else can do something, the chances are that you can do it, too. It may not be easy, but you can do it.

The trick to being as intelligent as someone else is to think like them. Richard Branson, Margaret Thatcher, Harrison Ford, Jean Michel Jarre, Jeffrey Archer, Stephen Tubs, Anita Roddick – most successful people have the same mental equipment as you do. They just use it differently. They've discovered a winning mental strategy for overcoming challenges. Biographies and interviews offer excellent insights into what kind of thinking leads to high-level accomplishment. You'll soon find that attitude – not raw intelligence – creates success. Of course, you may not want to be rich and famous. You may simply want to be a little more intelligent. There are many excellent books on how to improve your mental abilities. It may seem hard to get your brain round new problems at first, but always remember: you *have* the instrument. All you need is the right sort of practice.

Practice is the path to greater mental ability. The more your brain works in a certain way, the easier it is to work in that way again. If you want to remember historical dates, memorise historical dates, day in and day out, for months. If you want to write two-hour essays without your mind wandering, write dozens of two-hour essays. If you want to be calm in exams, take so many mock exams that, come exam day, you'll be too bored to get stressed. Practice makes perfect. It's that simple. At least it *should* be. Time and time again, people trying to improve their mental function can't get out of their own way. They know that they should practise, but they can't. Something inside shouts 'Why bother?' so loudly that they can't think. Self-confidence hypnotherapy can help, but the key to highly efficient mental function is relaxation.

When I was on the radio doing phone-in hypnosis, a caller named Mary complained that her memory was terrible. I asked her what she wanted to remember. 'Everything, really.' I told her no one can remember everything. Who'd want to? What would be the advantage of knowing the registration of every car you ever saw? How many people would like to remember where they spent every pound they've ever earned? If you *could* remember everything you saw, heard, felt, tasted and smelled, your mind would be so cluttered with useless information you couldn't make a cup of tea. I told Mary to close her eyes and imagine her last holiday. I asked her about her hotel room. Where was the radio? Were there any pictures on the wall? What did the room smell like? Once Mary relaxed, she remembered everything in exact detail. Her memory was perfect.

When you're relaxed, your mind is far more likely to recall information. Hold a gun to someone's head. Tell them they have ten seconds to remember their telephone number or you'll pull the trigger. Few people would make it. Sit them on a beautiful beach and ask the same question. They'd answer instantly. By the same token, when you're relaxed, you absorb information more easily. If you asked Mary to read a historical text in her hotel room one sunny afternoon, she'd recall far more factual material than if you sat her in the average school room. Add a dozen or so school children running riot around her, and the chances are she'd absorb practically nothing. To improve memory retention and replay, you need inner calm. You need to be able to relax your mind on command – no matter what the situation.

People who have difficulty studying and recalling information on demand are unable to find the mental calm they need for the job. They are neither focused nor relaxed. Hypnosis *is* focused relaxation. For smooth and efficient mental function, you can't do any better than a trance state. That's why subjects in a deep trance can recall information they were never even aware they knew. That's why people who *can* concentrate lose track of time, ignore outside sounds and forget about their own physical body. They are in a trance. Self-hypnosis will teach you how to put yourself into trance. You can then re-create this state on demand when you're 'awake'. It takes practice and dedication, but the rewards are enormous.

To take full advantage of self-hypnosis, it's important to realise that your mind can only think of one thing at a time. You can think of ten things in a second, but you can only think of them in order, one at a time. Concentration simply means staying with one train of thought for an extended period of time. A lack of concentration means constantly switching back and forth between unrelated subjects. That's another reason why so many people would fail the ten-second-give-me-your-phone-number-or-I'll-blow-your-head-off test. They would be so busy switching between thoughts about you, the gun, their imminent death and escape options that they wouldn't have the mental processing time to retrieve the number. Concentration requires a lack of competing stimuli – no school children running riot, no threat of death, no Guns 'n' Roses at 100 decibels. It also requires a different type of mental practice.

When you're practising concentrating, don't make the mistake of forcing yourself to concentrate. You have gently to train your mind to stick with a train of thought. First, convince your mind that the mental task ahead is more important than anything else you might want to think about. If your mind has to choose between thinking about what might happen on tomorrow night's date or another page of maths, you may be sunk before you begin. Spend at least two minutes with your eyes closed imagining the success of your mental efforts *before* you begin. See yourself completing the task successfully. Imagine earning some kind of reward: a compliment, exam result, new car, whatever. Try and recall the sense of peace and tranquillity you experienced somewhere beautiful.

If you can't concentrate on something longer than five minutes, don't fight it. Work for five minutes, take a break, then work for another five minutes, then take another break, and so on. At worst, you'll get the job done in five-minute bursts. At best, your concentration time will slowly increase as you 'forget' to be distracted. You'll gradually learn to use your brain with the stamina and expertise of a pro.

As for extraordinary mental abilities like photographic memory or total recall, there is considerable evidence that they are available to some people under hypnosis. The only way you'll know if your mind can achieve these feats is to try. Go for it. Find out what the trance state can do for you back here in 'the real world'. Explore the power of your imagination: the universe within the universe that is your inner mind. As there is no limit to the human imagination, there are no practical limits to what you can achieve. As long as you relax.

Controlling Pain

Before the discovery of painkillers and anaesthesia, surgeons were considered butchers, and for good reason. If the surgeon happened to remove what needed removing, if you were lucky enough to survive the sheer trauma of an operation, you'd probably die from infection. Before the turn of the century, somewhere between twenty-five and fifty per cent of all post-operative patients died from infection. Not all that surprising; surgeons used to wash their hands *after* surgery, not before. So what would you think if a Scottish surgeon in the 1840s went to India, learned hypnotism from the natives, eliminated his patients' pain, used hypnosis for over 3000 operations and reduced post-operative mortality to just five per cent? If you were the British Medical Association of the time, you'd put the surgeon on trial, revoke his licence and say that controlling pain was blasphemous. God intended people to suffer!

James Esdaile was a remarkable man. In an Empire built largely on greed and racial prejudice, the Scottish surgeon treated all patients alike. He never let his background or training blind him to a better way of carrying out his oath as a doctor. When he saw for himself the life-saving potential of mesmerism (the early name for hypnosis), Esdaile became its greatest champion. He was by no means the first to use hypnosis to eliminate pain; Esdaile had read of the technique long before his travels to India. But the good doctor put both career and reputation on the line in its defence. He lost both. It is only because of men like Esdaile that hypnotic pain control has not disappeared right off the map of Western medicine. This, despite the fact that hypnoanaesthesia boosts the immune system, whereas chemical anaesthesia lowers it.

Luckily, hypnotic pain control is available to you right here, right now. All you need is a little information and a lot of practice.

It's easy to believe that pain is simply nerve impulses from an injured body part, travelling through the nervous system to the brain. You bash your ankle, the nerves send a signal to your brain, and your ankle hurts. Pain is far more complicated than that. A bashed ankle creates acute or temporary pain. What about chronic pain? And why does the intensity of pain vary? When does discomfort become pain? Why do people have different abilities to withstand pain? What about the phantom limb pains experienced by people who've had a leg or arm amputated? There are psychosomatic pains, and referred pains that occur away from an injury. If you want to give yourself a headache, try to come up with a definition of pain that encompasses all these experiences.

Pain is an experience, not a series of nerve impulses. When you bash your ankle, the sensations coming from your ankle are interpreted, distorted and filtered by your brain. The same process applies to all other sensory information: sight, sound, taste and smell. Everyone experiences pain differently, just as everyone sees the Mona Lisa a little differently; and no two people hear Beethoven's Ninth in the same way. We all know our senses can lie. We can search high and low for something that's sitting on the table directly in front of us. We hear things that aren't there. Pain sensations can be equally deceptive. You can feel pain long after an injury has healed, and you can *not* feel pain when you are injured. Hypnosis can induce these effects. It can create visual and auditory hallucinations, and it can control the experience of pain. It can also remove pain completely.

Before you try hypnotic pain control, stop and consider if it's really such a good idea. Pain is Mother Nature's way of saying, hold on a minute, here's something that needs attention. If you didn't feel any pain, a ruptured appendix could claim your life without warning. Pain plays a life-saving role by alerting you to urgent or chronic physical problems. While physical pain isn't *always* related to a physical problem, it *usually* relates to something that needs fixing. You wouldn't want to walk around on a broken ankle, no matter how comfortable you felt. Before you begin to control or eliminate your pain, check with your doctor or specialist. If you're already on painkillers, start by supplementing your drugs rather than replacing them. If you're in any doubt at all, aim for pain control, not elimination.

One way to short-circuit the pain message is distraction. If you don't think about pain, you don't experience it. More precisely, if you concentrate on something *other* than your pain, you may be pain-free. Imagine you're in a hospital bed a few days after an operation. Something hurts like hell. Suddenly, the sexiest man or woman you've ever seen walks by. Even if it's just for a split second, your mind 'forgets' about the pain. This temporary interruption of your pain sensations is due to one of the fundamental limitations of the human mind: it can only think of one thing at a time. It can think of dozens of things in a second, but it can only think of them one at a time. Simply by focusing intensely on something pleasant, you can't think about – and therefore experience – the pain. Hypnosis makes this process even more powerful.

Confusion is another excellent pain-control technique. Most doctors giving children a jab ask them about their dog or teddy bear (distraction). Confusion is even more powerful. The doctor could say something like, 'Your arm may get a little cold now. At the same time, your other arm will start to get hotter. Or colder. Or maybe your toes will tingle. Do you feel a strange desire to eat chocolate biscuits?' The child is too confused to think about or feel the jab. To use this hypnotically, you set up 'crossed wires' in your subconscious mind. You can programme your inner mind so that whenever your right knee hurts, your left knee feels cold. Then, by rubbing your left thumb, the left knee warms up and the right knee stops throbbing. You confuse the mind about the location, intensity and 'cure' for your pain.

Sensory overload is another effective pain-control technique. Your mind can only handle so much sensory information – sight, sound, taste, touch or smell. When the mind is overloaded in one sensory area, the other senses are dulled. Put on a pair of headphones at the dentist's surgery and play an aria at full blast. Your mind will be unable to process other sensory inputs efficiently; you won't be so sensitive to what's going on in your mouth. If you have an aromatherapy massage, the powerful smells of the essential oils will dull physical pain. A sick person may be less aware of pain with extremely bright or perfumed flowers close by, because of their intense colour and smell. To use this technique hypnotically, you programme your inner mind to focus all its energy on a specific sense or command. Then, when you feel pain, you 'bliss out' on other, more pleasant sensations.

Ultimately, hypnosis *is* pain control. No matter which of these techniques you try, none is as simple and effective as simply putting yourself into a deep trance. When you're in deep trance, you leave your body behind. Even subjects who aren't using hypnosis for pain control routinely report distortions of bodily sensation. Typically, their arms and legs feel extremely heavy or large. Many subjects report a total lack of body awareness. Some even manage an out-of-body experience. With practice, you can use hypnosis to take control of your physical sensations. You can even create total numbness in a given part of your body, when necessary. (Pregnant women take note.) In short, deep hypnosis submerges your conscious mind beneath pain, to the inner ocean of calm and comfort within.

Better Sex

Sex is easy. Pleasure is difficult. Everyone knows roughly which bits go where and more or less what they're supposed to do. Very few people know how to find or sustain intense sexual pleasure – especially if they're in a long-term relationship. The biggest problem is routine. It's all too easy to slip into a predictable sexual pattern, a set physical and emotional progression from excitement to foreplay to orgasm to post-orgasm. People often find themselves doing the same things the same way, time after time, until they can plan the dinner while making love. While sexual routine is predictably pleasurable, it severely limits sexual satisfaction. You're trading dependability of supply for the possibility of pleasure. Safe sex, indeed.

There are plenty of books and videotapes that tell you how to spice up your sex life. An entire industry stands ready to help the sexually adventurous find stimulation. Once again, that's the easy bit. It's easy to discover new ways to do it, or new depictions of what you already like to do. If you want to change the way you get turned on, how you express your excitement, your potential for giving and receiving pleasure, and the intensity of orgasmic release, you have to change the way your brain works.

Sexual desire is a subconscious urge. How you feel and express that inner desire depends more on training than instinct. Whether it's a quickie in the back seat of a Cortina, or tender loving in a Parisian hotel room, your early sexual encounters create your sexual identity. A certain look in your lover's eye, the smell of a particular brand of perfume – these sensory experiences created strong stimulus–response programmes within your subconscious mind. They determine what turns you on. Through pleasurable repetition, your preference for sexual partner, pace, style, activity, position and more also become deeply ingrained habits. If these habits are too well fixed in your inner mind, if you stop adding new programmes, the sheer predictability of your subconscious desires and how you express them will eventually diminish the thrill. You get set in your ways, and that's *not* a recipe for a rich, rewarding sex life.

A client named Max came for hypnotherapy because he was stuck in a subconscious sexual habit. He could only achieve orgasm by having oral sex performed on him. Despite this restricted orgasmic pattern, Max and his wife enjoyed a full and varied sex life. However, when they wanted a child, Max's inability to achieve orgasm during penetrative sex became a problem. In the course of giving me his case history, Max told me his first girlfriend had refused to have intercourse, but really enjoyed giving and receiving oral sex. With his next lover, he explored all variety of penetrative sex positions, but delayed his orgasm until his penis was in her mouth. By his third lover, the orgasmic habit was so well-established he couldn't have an orgasm any other way – not even through masturbation. He lived with this limitation for twenty-seven years.

Max's subconscious mind was programmed to experience orgasmic release in response to a specific stimulus: the feeling of a woman's mouth around his penis. Through pleasurable repetition, the sexual habit became such a powerful subconscious programme that it precluded any other type of orgasmic experience. After his third hypnotherapy session, Max's inner mind was finally able to 'let go' of his oral sex programme long enough to absorb some new ideas. We were able to reprogramme his subconscious to appreciate more fully the varieties of sexual pleasure available to him, and to let these pleasures take him to orgasm. It worked. Max now has a young son. Equally important, his sex life has improved dramatically. Max can masturbate to orgasm again, and ejaculate in almost any position he or his wife choose.

Women who can't climax can probably identify with Max's restricted subconscious programme. Some women find orgasms too difficult to achieve, and resign themselves to the fact that their body/mind can only experience so much pleasure. Some of them have never experienced *any* type of orgasm. Using self-hypnosis, a woman can reprogramme her subconscious so she can experience even what she's never experienced before: clitoral, vaginal or even multiple orgasms. By the same token, a man can reprogramme himself to postpone his orgasm (without having to concentrate on football scores). Both sexes can use hypnosis simply to reprogramme themselves for heightened pleasure. As your subconscious mind controls the vast majority of your physical, mental and emotional responses to sexual stimuli, the possibilities are endless.

Our sexual habits are not carved in stone; they're programmed into our subconscious mind. Hypnosis offers you the chance to change your subconscious sexual habits for increased sexual pleasure. Of course, there are at least as many ideas of 'increased sexual pleasure' as there are pornographic magazines for sale in Amsterdam. As with all hypnotic re-programming, you need to start with a clear idea of what you want to achieve. Some lovers might like to use hypnosis to increase their sexual confidence and/or desirability. Stronger orgasms may increase pleasure, or perhaps a faster recovery time. Let your imagination be your guide. There are few things as sexy as your lover's pleasure, so why not ask your partner(s) what *they* would like to change about your routine. What can be conceived can be created.

If you're still a little dubious about using hypnosis to change your sexual responses, remember that sex *is* hypnotic. Have you ever lost track of time during sex? Didn't hear the phone ring? Felt your body become somehow stronger and more responsive? After orgasm, are your senses somehow sharper? Is your mind calmer and clearer? If you answer yes to any of these questions, you've already experienced a state of mind with all the characteristics of a hypnotic trance: time distortion, extreme mental focus, enhanced creativity and deep physical and mental relaxation. Since you're in a trance or trance-like state when you're having sex, why not refine and improve that mental state? It's the perfect time to experiment with new possibilities, or trigger pre-planned hypnotic programmes.

Experimenting with your sexuality, opening yourself up to the rich variety of sexual expression within yourself, improves your enjoyment of your life force. Studies prove time and time again that people with an active sex life are healthier, happier and live longer than those who are sexually inactive or frustrated. The inescapable truth is that we *are* sexual beings. If we leave our sexual programming to the vagaries of chance, if we simply accept the end result of this programming and say, 'That's it, that's me, that's what I'm like', we're missing an opportunity to improve the quality of our life.

Part Four

THE GENTLE ART OF SELF-HYPNOSIS

'If you want to shoot ducks, go where the ducks are.'

Peter Farago

(my father)

11

Exploding the Myths

In the public imagination, a hypnotist is a man with piercing eyes and a pocket watch. He swings his watch, your eyes droop and you fall into a trance. He can then get you to do anything – from clucking like a chicken to . . . something dark and sinister. Hypnosis as a black art is a common theme of books and films. In a popular novel, a man named Svengali puts an impressionable young girl under his hypnotic spell. The tale was so compelling that we now call someone with a seemingly supernatural hold on others a 'Svengali'. In the film, *The Manchurian Candidate*, Russian baddies use hypnosis to turn a squad of captured American soldiers into unwitting assassins, activated by a single phone call. The message is clear: mess with hypnosis, and you're messing with something dangerous.

If you buy this myth, it's not just Hollywood that's to blame. Stage hypnotists and even some hypnotherapists are slow to discourage public ignorance and fear. It pulls in the punters, intimidates subjects and discourages competition. The truth about hypnosis is far more down to earth than the mythmakers would have you believe. Hypnosis is not black magic. It's a practical skill. You don't have to be 'born with the power'. You don't need years of training with a guru or psychologist. With a little guidance and practice, almost anyone can learn to hypnotise a willing subject. Anyone with the desire can put themselves into a hypnotic trance. Self-hypnosis is not about dabbling with the dark side. It's about stepping into the light and taking control of your life.

To master self-hypnosis, you need to approach the technique with an open mind. The following questions and answers will help explode some of the common misconceptions surrounding hypnosis. Abandon these myths and you'll lose your ignorance and fear. With calm confidence, you can then delve deep enough into your inner mind to make the changes you need to make to change your life. If you're still slightly mystified after reading this chapter, good. Self-hypnosis is a way to explore and modify your subconscious mind. As the subconscious is a world unto itself, this exploration is bound to raise a world of new questions. In hypnosis, as in the rest of life, there will always be unanswered questions. Which is exactly how it should be.

What is hypnosis? Do you go to sleep?

Ever since the word hypnosis became widely used, people have debated its meaning. Is hypnosis a shift from reality into the world of dreams, a change in brain chemistry or simply an elaborate game of let's pretend? Who knows? Defining this state of mind is like trying to describe your favourite piece of music. You can explain the chord progression, list the instruments, compare the sound to beautiful vistas, explain its effect on your emotions and even hand over the sheet music. Nothing will ever compare to sitting a person down and playing them the piece through a stereo. Even then, they may not hear the music in the same way as you. After hypnotising hundreds of clients, I can state without reservation that they all experience hypnosis in a different and deeply personal way. Hypnosis means something different to every one.

What will hypnosis be like for you? You may already know the answer. People slip into a hypnotic state – a 'trance' – on a regular basis. Have you ever lost track of time while driving? Have you ever shared the emotions of a hero or heroine in a film? Have you ever been so preoccupied with something you didn't hear someone calling you? Driving, films and hobbies can all create a naturally occurring trance. This mental state features time distortion (time seems to move faster or slower), emotional suggestibility (your emotions are easily triggered), extreme concentration (you focus on one thing to the complete exclusion of everything else), and sensory distortion (your senses 'lie' to you). People often slip into a hypnotic trance when reading a good book, praying, dancing, driving or making love – anything that 'takes them away from it all'. In two words, hypnosis is focused relaxation.

Most people equate hypnosis with sleep because hypnotised subjects on stage or in movies look like they're asleep. They seem 'gone' or 'dead to the world'. The hypnotist plays to this belief by using the word 'sleep' to induce trance and 'wake up' to end it. The fact that some subjects can't remember what's happened reinforces the mistaken idea that they were asleep. Hypnotised subjects look like they're asleep because they're very, very relaxed. They forget what's happened because the hypnotist commands them to forget – a hypnotic effect called induced amnesia. Also keep in mind that a stage hypnotist selects the most suggestible subjects he or she can find. These sub-

jects quickly enter a deep trance and respond completely. No matter
how strange their behaviour, they are not asleep. Nor are they repre-
sentative of the general population.

Hypnosis is not sleep. When you're in a trance, you don't blank out
or lose consciousness like you would during general anaesthesia or a
deep sleep. You're fully awake and alert, but mentally and physically
relaxed. For hypnosis to work properly, you *must* be awake. If you're
inner mind is sleeping, it can't focus on new ideas and suggestions. As
for self-hypnosis, how could you possibly be your own hypnotist if
you're asleep? In fact, many people emerge from trance and say, 'I
wasn't hypnotised. I didn't feel "out of it" or asleep.' Never forget that
the importance of trance is not what it feels like, but what you can do
with it.

Can anyone be hypnotised?

Yes, anyone can be hypnotised. All human beings have a natural ability to enter a hypnotic state. The best subjects tend to be young people
with an active imagination and a willingness to respond to authority.
The only people who may be completely un-hypnotisable are the
severely mentally handicapped or disturbed. However . . .

It's impossible to make generalisations about hypnotic ability.
Susceptibility – a subject's ability to be deeply hypnotised – varies
from person to person. Not all people can be hypnotised straight off.
Some people easily enter a deep trance, while others take a long time
to enter a light trance. Some people need a deep trance to make a
change or follow a command, while others will respond completely in
a light trance. Some people respond well to one hypnotist, but not
another. Some people respond to one hypnotic technique, but not
another. To top it all off, some people don't even know when they've
been hypnotised!

At the end of the day, the only people who are impossible to hypnotise are people who don't want to be hypnotised. Luckily for professional hypnotists, these people don't come on stage or into therapy.
They also don't buy books on self-hypnosis. Which suggests that you
have an excellent chance of putting yourself into a deep trance.

But don't get hung up on whether or not you can achieve a deep
trance. Self-hypnosis is a no-lose situation. As long as you keep at it,
failure is impossible. You will eventually achieve the trance depth you
need to change your subconscious habits. But even if you can't hypnotise yourself, or hypnotise yourself to some pre-conceived idea of a
'deep enough trance', it really doesn't matter. You're still learning to
relax every day and telling yourself positive things about yourself.

Often, that's more than enough to create the positive change you're looking for.

Can a subject be hypnotised to do something 'against their will'?

Most hypnotists will tell you that a person under hypnosis will not follow an amoral command. It's the hypnotist's standard response to this question, and it's just about true. Under most circumstances, a hypnotised person will not follow an amoral or illegal command. But rarely it can happen. The likelihood of following an unnatural command depends on the subject's level of susceptibility (how deeply they can be hypnotised), what they are asked to do (how uncomfortable the command seems) and where they are (in front of an audience or in private). Even the most upright citizen can be tricked into dangerous, unethical or illegal acts under hypnosis.

For example, if a hypnotist wants a subject to steal a purse, he wouldn't say, 'When you wake up you will go over and steal Mary's blue purse from her handbag.' He would say, 'The blue purse in Mary's handbag is your purse. When you wake up you will go over and take your blue purse out of Mary's handbag and put it into your handbag.' The subject is fooled into doing something against their will. Most hypnotists insist a subject's moral code is stronger than hypnotic command; they simply wake up if asked to do something against their will. Have these hypnotists tried the handbag experiment? What about stage hypnotists? Do all of their subjects really want to make fools of themselves in front of an audience?

That said, chances of encountering an evil hypnotist are very slim indeed. Someone practising self-hypnosis doesn't need to worry about the possibility of hypnotic manipulation. You're not likely to use hypnosis to force yourself to do something you don't want to do. For one thing, it's too confusing; if you didn't want to do something, you wouldn't hypnotise yourself to do it. For another, if you genuinely believe you have two separate personalities who are at war with each other, you probably won't be able to hypnotise yourself (and should seek professional help). However, the fear of being hypnotised to do something evil or amoral is what gives hypnosis its slightly sinister reputation. It's important to shed a little light on this darkened corner, so you can see hypnosis for what it is: a simple tool for personal transformation.

Will self-hypnosis work for me?

You need two things to succeed in self-hypnosis: desire and discipline. Generally speaking, people who have enough desire to succeed at self-hypnosis are people with problems. As a hypnotherapist, I see people who want to use hypnosis to overcome what they perceive to be a crisis situation. They've tried living with their problem, sometimes for years, and failed. Most clients have tried other therapeutic approaches such as their doctor or a diet, also without success. By the time they get to the clinic they're fed up with their problem. The situation has become so intolerable that they desperately want to change. Their desire to be hypnotised is great, because they want it to work. As a result, it doesn't take much to hypnotise them, and the results are often impressive. If you're well and truly fed up with your particular problem, you're motivated enough to succeed with self-hypnosis.

You don't *have* to be in crisis to do well with self-hypnosis. People looking for spiritual adventure or simple self-improvement also have sufficient desire to make self-hypnosis work. These are people who find that their normal state of mind simply isn't exciting or meaningful enough to make them happy. They hunger for something more powerful and interesting than everyday reality. By using self-hypnosis to tap into their inner mind, they can plug into the endlessly fascinating world of their own imagination. Exploring this inner world makes their normal world more tolerable. When they discover that they can use the peace of their inner world to change their lives in the 'real' world, they embark on the adventure of a lifetime.

Whatever brings you to self-hypnosis, you need discipline to make it work. Like any other skill, from cooking to Calypso, hypnotic ability improves with practice. The more you hypnotise yourself, the easier it becomes. With time, you begin to sense that you know what you're doing. This feeling of confidence leads to deeper trances and better results. Deeper trances and better results encourage you, the hypnotist, to keep at it. Stick with it and you'll quickly find yourself getting better and better.

12

Can I Be Hypnotised?

There is no reliable way to predict a person's ability to be hypnotised. Certain rules *seem* to apply, such as the younger you are, the easier you are to hypnotise. Then you come across a ten-year-old who responds like a block of cement, or an 82-year-old grandmother who will go so deeply into trance she can't remember what happened (spontaneous amnesia). Stage hypnotists rely on their subjects to be self-selecting. They expect that anyone who comes on stage to be hypnotised wants to be hypnotised so much that they're capable of a deep trance. The stage hypnotist is usually right, but even the best will admit that there are those rare and terrible nights when not a single volunteer responds well. There is no general rule about who can and can not be easily hypnotised.

The only way to know is to test. This chapter contains several tests which will help establish your general level of hypnotisability.

Suggestability Test

Start with this simple test. Circle A, B or C.

1. Close your eyes and imagine yourself at a movie. How clearly can you picture your favourite actor or actress?
    (A) Easily (B) Vaguely (C) Can't 'get it'

2. You're on a diet and you're bored. There's a chocolate bar in the cupboard. Will you
    (A) Finish it (B) Take one bite (C) Leave it there

3. Do you ever cry while watching a sad movie on TV?
    (A) Sometimes (B) Rarely (C) Never

4. Imagine a place where you were happy. How well can you re-experience it?
    (A) Well (B) So-so (C) Barely

5. *If you drive,* have you ever missed your exit on the motorway?
   (A) More than once (B) Once (C) Never

   If you don't drive, do you ever find yourself losing track of time?
   (A) Frequently (B) Sometimes (C) Never

6. Generally speaking, how long does it take you to fall asleep?
   (A) About ten minutes (B) Closer to half an hour (C) At least an hour

7. Imagine you're in love. How vivid is your image or feeling?
   (A) Very vivid (B) Somewhat vivid (C) Not clear at all

8. You're last off a bus and you find a wallet filled with money. Assuming your intentions are honest, you'd
   (A) Take it to the driver (B) Take it to the police (C) Take it and call the owner

9. You daydream
   (A) A lot (B) From time to time (C) Rarely, if ever

10. Think about a proud moment of personal triumph. Close your eyes and try to re-experience it. It was
    (A) Easy to re-experience (B) Fairly difficult (C) Difficult or impossible

Scoring

Give yourself 10 points for each A answer,
5 for each B and 0 for each C.

55–100   You have a great imagination; you trust and let go. You're a natural for self-hypnosis and reaping its benefits.

25–54   Once you get past your analytical approach and tap into your imagination, self-hypnosis will become easier for you.

0–24   You have a very analytical mind and fear giving up control. Learning how to 'let go' through self-hypnosis will be of immense benefit.

The following run-down explains the scoring in more detail, so you can get a better idea of what qualities make a person hypnotic . . .

Question 1: Picture your favourite actor . . .

Your imagination is the bridge between your conscious and subconscious mind. People who have a well-developed visual imagination are more likely to respond to hypnotic programming because they can literally 'see' the positive future ahead. This vision of change inspires the subconscious to accept new ideas.

Question 2: Eat the chocolate?

People without 'will-power' are actually *more* hypnotic than people who can resist temptation. Will-power comes from the rational mind; you resist something because it 'makes sense' not to do it. If a subject's subconscious urges are stronger than their rational mind, it reveals a very powerful inner mind.

Question 3: Crying at a sad movie

People who cry at sad movies tend to have greater access to their emotional core: their subconscious mind. Also, empathy with the emotions of others indicates an inner mind that's receptive to new ways of looking at the world.

Question 4: Re-experience a happy place . . .

The easiest way to create a specific state of mind is to re-create it – to remember a place or time where you experienced the same feeling. Think of a beautiful beach and you're relaxed. Think of a traffic jam and you're tense. Someone who can vividly recall pleasant experiences finds it easier to create the relaxed and receptive state of mind called hypnosis.

Question 5: Missed exit, lost time . . .

Drivers who miss their motorway exit are usually in a naturally occurring trance state. The same is true for people who lose track of time. In both cases, the person is awake but relaxed. They're so relaxed that their conscious mind literally 'forgets' about concepts like time and distance. In trance, concepts like time and space are entirely subjective and flexible.

Question 6: How long to fall asleep?

Although hypnosis is not sleep, the amount of time it takes to fall asleep is a good measure of your ability to relax. If you can relax quickly and deeply at the end of the day, you should be able to train yourself to relax quickly and deeply during self-hypnosis. Also, most people who have trouble sleeping are troubled by worry and doubt. For a good trance, you have to set all your problems to one side.

Question 7: Imagine you're in love

Love is even harder to define than hypnosis. Even so, people in love and people in trance experience many of the same mental 'disturbances': time distortion, a feeling of liberation, high emotions and an awareness of the beauty in everyday life. If you can vividly recall being in love, you probably enjoyed it immensely. Which means you'll enjoy and appreciate the trance state as well.

Question 8: Finding a wallet on a bus

If you return the wallet to the driver, this shows that you feel very comfortable with authority. You don't mind surrendering your control of the situation to someone else. In self-hypnosis, you are the authority figure to your subconscious mind. People who respond well to outside authority usually have a subconscious mind that's willing to accept new 'orders'.

Question 9: Daydreaming

Daydreaming is a form of light hypnosis. Or hypnosis is a deep form of daydreaming. Whichever way you look at it, people who like to drift off into a world of their own will *love* drifting off into hypnosis.

Question 10: Re-experiencing personal triumph

This question measures the strength of your (subconscious) imagination, but it also tests your level of self-confidence. If you're generally confident about your ability to succeed at things, you're more likely to stick with self-hypnosis long enough to succeed.

Self-hypnosis is the art of exploring and altering your subconscious mind. As your subconscious mind doesn't 'think', any rational test only gives you a vague idea of your hypnotic ability. So that's it for the intellectual approach. The rest of the tests are experiential – you have to do them. No matter what results you achieve, *keep repeating the test*. Try the tests at different times of day. Try them with friends. Try them alone. Try them when you're tired or excited or happy or sad. Try each one *at least* ten times. Master these tests and you're well on your way to mastering self-hypnosis.

Hand–Magnet Test

First, memorise the following hypnotic script:

'My right hand is a powerful magnet. My left hand is a piece of metal. My right hand is attracted to my left hand. My right hand and left hand are moving closer and closer. Closer and closer. Closer and closer. Closer and closer. Closer and closer. Etc.'

Once you've committed that script to memory, stand in a comfortable position with your arms by your sides. Take a few seconds to relax. Shake your arms and legs a bit to release physical tension from your body. Take a couple of deep breaths, then let the air out slowly. When you're ready, stand with your feet slightly apart. Hold both arms up straight out from your body at shoulder height. (You should look like a sleepwalker or someone about to start a high dive.) Turn your hands so your palms are facing each other, no more than one foot apart. Close your eyes. Repeat the hand–magnet script out loud . . .

> 'My right hand is a powerful magnet. My left hand is a piece of metal. My right hand is attracted to my left hand. My right hand and left hand are moving closer and closer. Closer and closer. Closer and closer. Closer and closer. Closer and closer. Etc.'

Keep saying 'closer and closer' until your hands touch – even if it takes all day. When your hands touch, open your eyes and look at your hands. Then put them down. The test is finished . . . Check and see how you rate. Then read the suggestions below under 'Advanced Techniques for the Hand–Magnet Test' and try again. And again. Do the test at least ten times, at different times of day and in different situations.

Scoring the Hand–Magnet Test

• **If your hands move towards each other in jerky movements in less than thirty seconds,** if you feel a magnetic force between your hands pulling them together, you are highly hypnotic. Your subconscious mind is responding to an imaginary suggestion by creating a physical response (moving your hands).

• **If your hands move in towards each other in jerky movements, but it takes longer than sixty seconds for them to touch,** you're also hypnotic, but you'll need more practice.

• **If your hands move quickly together in one smooth movement,** you're responding consciously – not hypnotically. Try again, but don't consciously move your hands. Simply 'let' them move together when you feel something happening.

• **If nothing happens,** don't worry. Some people are better at a full session of self-hypnosis than at quick hypnotic tests. Learning self-hypnosis is like learning any other skill: persistence is *always* more important than talent. Keep trying the tests until you can feel something. If you get frustrated, ask someone you respect to read the instructions to you.

Advanced Techniques for the Hand–Magnet Test

Self-hypnosis is like playing the blues. Most people can learn to play basic blues on a piano in about fifteen minutes. It then takes them the rest of their life to master the blues. If you can get your hands to move together fairly quickly in the hand–magnet test, congratulations! You've learned how to hypnotise yourself. All you need to do now is learn how to do it *better*. If you're having trouble getting your hands to touch, you're in exactly the same situation: you know how to do it, but you need to do it better. Whether you're a natural or a late bloomer, improvement means experimenting with the two most important elements of self-hypnosis: hypnotic voice and effective suggestion.

Whether you say the hand–magnet script out loud or silently to yourself, there's a specific tone to the voice you use to talk to yourself. Hypnotists' voices tend to fall into two different camps: the 'mother' or the 'father'. (This is not intended as a sexist classification system. Obviously, both men and women are fully capable of using either a 'mother' or 'father' hypnotic voice.) The mother voice is the caring, nurturing voice. Hypnotists who use this voice speak to the subconscious mind in a kind, gentle and loving way. They treat the inner mind as a slow but ever-so-sweet five-year-old. The father voice is the more stern and commanding voice. It is also loving, but in an iron-fist-in-a-velvet-glove sort of way. Hypnotists who use the father voice also regard the inner mind as a five-year-old child, but a five-year-old who has a history of being naughty if you turn your back for too long.

Most hypnotists make the mistake of using only one of these voices. Just as a child needs both love and discipline, your inner mind needs a combination of gentle nurturing and direct command. Right from the start, use both voices. Try the hand–magnet test being really syrupy sweet to yourself. Then try it again being totally stern and forceful. Then try it again starting with the mother voice and switching to the father voice. There are a hundred different ways to say the words 'closer and closer'. Find the best way to say these words that makes your hands move together, but don't think of it as *the* hypnotic voice. Just as a composer needs more than one instrument to make beautiful music, a self-hypnotist needs more than one hypnotic voice to 'play' his or her subconscious mind.

No matter what hypnotic voice you use, you need to give yourself effective suggestions. Some inner minds respond best to commands that appeal to the visual sense. Others need a bit of a 'plot' to get their imagination (subconscious) involved. And others need as many different suggestions as possible. Once you've successfully completed the hand–magnet test a few times using the script as written, add some new ideas. Try visual suggestions like, 'My hands are moving together like two cars heading for the same parking place.' Try plot lines like, 'I've been put under a strange spell by a sorcerer. My right hand is now a magnet . . .' Try intensifying the sensations with, 'Just like a real magnet and a real piece of metal, the closer my hands get, the stronger the force becomes.' Try combining different ideas. Use your imagination and you can't go wrong.

The Balloon–Sand Test

First, as best you can, memorise the following script:

> 'My right hand is resting on a helium balloon. The balloon is filling with gas. The balloon is getting lighter and lighter. My right hand is rising higher and higher.
>
> 'My left hand is holding a bag of sand. The bag is filling with sand. The sand is getting heavier and heavier. My left hand is sinking lower and lower.
>
> 'Right hand, lighter. Left hand, heavier. Lighter and heavier. Heavier and lighter. Lighter and heavier. Heavier and lighter. Etc.'

Next, stand comfortably, shake off any tension and take a couple of deep breaths. Raise your arms and hold them straight out from your body at shoulder height. This time, turn your right hand so the palm faces down. Turn your left hand so the palm faces up. Close your eyes. Repeat the balloon–sand script, either out loud or silently to yourself . . .

Keep at it until you think your hands are far apart. Then open your eyes, look at your arms and put them down.

Scoring the Balloon–Sand Test

• **If both hands rise and fall in irregular movements within thirty seconds,** you're highly hypnotic.

• **If both hands rise and fall in irregular movements within sixty seconds,** you're getting there, but still need more practice.

• **If your left hand seems to fall faster than the right hand rises up,** that's completely normal. Gravity and muscle strain are helping the left hand to sink down.

- **If your hands rise and fall in a smooth movement,** try again. Don't force it – let it happen.

- **If nothing happens,** don't worry. The slowest starters are often the most enthusiastic subjects once they get the knack. Try the new suggestions below.

Advanced Techniques for the Balloon–Sand Test

We don't consciously control the pace of our speech in everyday conversation. The rate that words come out of our mouth does vary – we speak faster if we're nervous or slower if we're drunk – but it's not something we think about. Yet the pace at which people speak to us can have a profound effect. It's hard to concentrate if a person speaks too quickly. You can become terribly bored if a person speaks too slowly. A well-timed pause can tell you more than the most eloquent speech. By varying the pace at which you speak to yourself during self-hypnosis, you can significantly improve the effectiveness of the suggestions.

There's no magic speaking rate. You need to discover what works best for you. Try repeating the script as fast as you can. This technique can overload the rational mind and produce impressive results. Then try saying the script very, very, slowly. Believe it or not, boredom is a highly effective hypnotic technique. The rational mind is so bored with the suggestions, it wanders off. The always-listening subconscious mind can then get on with the job of raising and lowering your hands. Also try starting slowly, then speeding up. And don't forget to play with the other variables: hypnotic voice and creative suggestion. Should you use the mother voice when you're speaking slowly, then switch to a rapid-fire father voice? What new ideas will make the test more powerful? Experiment and see.

Finger-Raise Test

First, memorise this script:

> 'I'm staring directly at the X on my hand. Nothing else matters but the X on my hand. As I stare at the X on my hand, my index finger is getting lighter and lighter. My finger is rising up. My finger is getting lighter and lighter. My finger is rising up. My finger is getting lighter and lighter. My finger is rising up. Etc.'

Now sit down somewhere comfortable next to a table or desk. Ideally, the top of the desk or table should be slightly lower than your nipples. Place one of your arms on the desk or table, so that the hand rests comfortably on the surface. *Make sure your entire arm up to the elbow is on the table so you don't cut off the circulation to your hand.*

Take a pen and make a small X on the top of your hand. The best spot is in the middle of your hand, between the thumb and index finger (on the thumb muscle). Stare directly at the centre of the X. Take a couple of deep breaths, exhaling slowly. Repeat the script silently to yourself. Keep repeating the script until your finger rises off the desk or table. When the finger starts to lift off, change the script. Say to yourself:

'The higher up my finger rises up, the more relaxed I feel. Lighter and lighter. The higher up my finger rises up, the more relaxed I feel. Lighter and lighter. Etc.'

When your index finger has risen well above the rest of your fingers, close your eyes. Then take a deep breath in. Exhale and drop your finger. Enjoy breathing normally for a bit, then open your eyes.

Scoring the Finger-Raise Test

• **If your finger jerks upwards within sixty seconds,** you're highly hypnotic.

• **If your finger jerks upwards after more than sixty seconds,** you're also hypnotic, but need to work on your technique.

• **If your finger rises up quickly in a smooth movement,** you're moving the finger consciously. Try again, but don't *make* it happen. Play around with different techniques and *let* it happen.

• **If your finger doesn't rise up,** don't worry. Try altering the various elements of self-hypnosis, as well as the time and situation. Go back and try the other tests. Have someone read the script(s) to you. If you're still not getting any results, forget it. Move on to the next chapters and learn full self-hypnosis. Some people just don't do well at tests.

Advanced Techniques for the Finger-Raise Test

The finger-raise script contains an important hypnotic technique called a feedback loop. You link one subconscious reaction (finger rising) to another (relaxation). Since success gives the subconscious confidence, one successful subconscious response leads to another. Experiment with the loop. First, intensify the effect by adding:

'The higher my finger rises up, the more hypnotic I feel. The more hypnotic I feel, the higher my finger rises up.'

Then try changing the second hypnotic response to something physical, like:

'The higher my finger rises up, the heavier my eyelids feel.'

Try linking it to a modest, measurable goal, like:

'The higher my finger rises up, the easier it is to smoke one less cigarette a day.'

Or:

'The higher my finger rises up, the easier it is to do self-hypnosis.'

Let's Do It! Go For Trance

In addition to continuing to experiment with hypnotic voice, creative suggestion, pace and feedback loops, you can now experiment with the trance state itself. When you finally close your eyes, take a deep breath, exhale and drop your finger and you've entered a trance. For some, it will be a very light trance. Others will enter a medium trance. At this point, all you should do is enjoy it. Just remain still and silent for as long as you can. Let your mind drift. See where it takes you. The worst that can happen is that you may fall asleep. (If you do, you'll wake up as normal.) The best that can happen is . . . who knows?

By now, you probably realise that successful self-hypnosis requires a number of different skills. Some of these you'll learn from this text. Others you'll pick up by practice and simple intuition. No matter where you are on the learning curve, don't spend too much time analysing your performance. The goal of self-hypnosis is to let go of your cares and worries and doubts – not add to them. So relax and enjoy the ride . . .

13

Practising Self-Hypnosis

Take a deep breath. Go on, take a nice deep breath. Let the air out slowly. There are a lot of ways to enter into a hypnotic trance, but the fastest way to change your consciousness is to change your breathing. For self-hypnosis, the best type of breathing is relaxed breathing – *not deep breathing*. Relaxed breathing is slow breathing. When I hypnotise a woman for painless childbirth, we try to get her breathing down to no more than six breaths per minute. Relaxed breathing is even breathing. Every breath is exactly the same as the one before and the one after. Relaxed breathing is physically comfortable breathing. Every breath makes maximum use of the lungs without over-straining the chest or abdominal muscles. Relaxed breathing is the key to the door of your subconscious.

Slow, regular breathing creates several important hypnotic effects. First, you relax. Although it is possible to enter a hypnotic state by breathing rapidly (hyperventilating), it's not as pleasant or effective as calming your body. When you're in a normal relaxed frame of mind, you automatically breathe slowly and evenly. By relaxing your breathing you trigger this pre-existing programme. The new breathing pattern sends a clear message to your subconscious mind to relax. Second, relaxed breathing frees your subconscious mind. Breathing is one of the primary body functions controlled by the subconscious. When you breathe consciously, the subconscious has less 'work' to do. It becomes more receptive. And lastly, relaxed breathing focuses your conscious mind. If you're concentrating on your breathing, you can't think of anything else. You block out the background noise preventing deep relaxation and trance.

A little breathing practice takes you a long way towards deep trance. To help you concentrate on your breathing, use the following breathing script. Don't bother memorising the script word for word. Read it here ten times, or until you can remember the four basic ideas. Try starting this exercise with the Finger-Raise Test (see page 111). If you're a little unsure of your memory or just want to try another approach, record the script on to a tape, close your eyes and listen. Don't spend more than ten minutes at any one time on this exercise.

Relaxed Breathing Script

1. Easy breathing

Close your eyes. Now relax your breathing. The goal is not deep breathing, but easy breathing. So make your breathing as easy and relaxed as possible. Breathe nice and easy and relaxed. And as you relax your breathing, you will relax. Deeper and deeper relaxed with each breath out.

2. Comfortable muscles

The only muscles that you're moving in your whole body are the muscles you're using to breathe. Feel exactly which muscles you're using. Relax those muscles. Breathe in the most comfortable way possible. Deeper and deeper relaxed, with each breath out.

3. Amount of air

Imagine you can feel every molecule of air flowing in, and flowing out, of your body. Breathe in, and let out, the perfect amount of air. The perfect amount of air you need to relax. Deeper and deeper relaxed with each breath out.

4. Breathing rate

Adjust the rate, or speed, of your breathing. Make every breath exactly the same. The same as the one before. The same as the one after. Every breath exactly the same. Every breath relaxed. Deeper and deeper relaxed with each breath out.

Advanced Breathing Exercise

Try the exercise again. This time experiment with your hypnotic voice, pace and creative suggestions. For example, this script uses the word 'you'. Talking to your inner mind as a separate part of yourself is an excellent way to get to grips with your subconscious 'personality'. Some people find it a bit strange at first. Try substituting the personal pronoun 'I' and see if it's more effective. There is also considerable scope for creativity. Let the key word in each part of the exercise suggest images, sensations and ideas which you can add to the script. Alter the suggestions below and/or come up with your own that are personally appealing – whatever *you* think is powerful. Be specific! For example:

1. 'Easy'

Make your breathing as easy as walking down ____ ˊ (a beautiful beach).
   Make your breathing as easy as two plus two.
   Make your breathing as easy as smelling ____ (favourite perfume).

2. 'Comfortable'

Breathe as comfortably as talking to ____ (an old friend).
   Breathe as comfortably as walking through ____ (favourite park).
   Breathe as comfortably as snuggling up to ____.

3. 'Amount'

Breathe in the perfect amount of air, like drinking the perfect amount of ____ (favourite drink).
   Breathe in the perfect amount of air, like running a bath at the perfect temperature.
   Breathe in the perfect amount of air, like ____ (favourite singer) singing the perfect note.

4. 'Rate'

Make every breath the same, like perfect waves, rolling into the shore.
   Make every breath the same, like an endless line of ____ (favourite biscuit or cracker).
   Make every breath the same, like slowly signing your name over and over again.

Progressive Relaxation Exercise

If you've been in a drama or dance class, you've probably come across a progressive relaxation exercise. The aim of the exercise is to slowly relax every part of your physical body. You shift your consciousness to each part of the body and 'will' it to relax. Although progressive relaxation is used mostly to increase physical relaxation and control, it's an extremely hypnotic technique. Progressive relaxation focuses the mind *and* trains the subconscious to respond to your command. By practising this technique, you will learn to ease mental and physical tension. Even more important, you will create a receptive frame of mind for hypnotic reprogramming.

You'll need to find somewhere really comfortable for this exercise – *but don't lie down!* We all have a subconscious programme for when we lie down with our eyes closed called 'sleep', and you can't practise self-hypnosis if you're asleep. If you decide to use your bed, prop your-self up with some pillows so your back is supported by the headboard or wall.

When you're settled in, read the following script, relaxing each body part as you read. Then try it with your eyes closed. If you need to, record the script and play it back.

Progressive Relaxation Script

I am now beginning to relax. Relaxing deeper and deeper with each breath out. Breathing nice and easy and relaxed.

I am now imagining a wave of perfect relaxation just above my head. It may be a warming wave. It may be a cooling wave. It may be a wave that simply releases my physical tension. I can imagine this wave of perfect relaxation just above my head.

The wave is coming down over my head. Relaxing my forehead and head perfectly. My forehead and head feel nice and relaxed.

The wave of perfect relaxation is flowing down a little further, over my eyes and ears and nose. My eyes and ears and nose are relaxing. Wave coming down a bit more, relaxing my mouth. Teeth. And gums. And now my jaw. The wave of perfect relaxation is relaxing all the tension in my jaw. My jaw can now relax as my teeth part just a little and I relax.

The wave of perfect relaxation is flowing down now in to my neck and shoulders. Relaxing my neck and shoulders perfectly. All the ten-sion and stress draining out of my neck and shoulders. Nice and loose and relaxed.

The wave of perfect relaxation spreading down now into both arms. Relaxing both biceps. Relaxing both forearms. Flowing down into my wrists. Relaxing my wrists. And now my fingers. Both arms, from the shoulders to my fingertips, perfectly relaxed and comfortable.

The wave of perfect relaxation flowing down into my back. Flowing down my spine. Relaxing every muscle, every fibre, every cell of my back. My entire back is wonderfully comfortable. Perfectly relaxed.

The wave of perfect relaxation is spreading down my chest now. Relaxing my heart. And lungs. And stomach. All my internal organs are nice and loose and limp and relaxed.

The wave of perfect relaxation passing through my lower body into the long muscles of my thighs. My thigh muscles are relaxing, like loose and floppy rubber bands. Thigh muscles relaxed.

The wave of perfect relaxation going into my knees. Sinking straight into my knees. Soothing and bathing my knees in perfect relaxation. My knees are nice and warm and relaxed.

Waves of perfect relaxation flowing into both calves. Calf muscles letting go as they relax more and more. More and more relaxed.

The wave of perfect relaxation spreading into my feet. My feet are relaxing. All the bones and muscles and tendons in my feet relaxing deeply. My feet feel perfectly relaxed.

I am now perfectly relaxed. From head . . . to toe . . . perfectly relaxed. Wonderfully comfortable. When I'm ready to wake up, I'll count to three. When I wake up, I will remain. Perfectly relaxed. One, two, three.

Advanced Relaxation Exercise

As always, once you've mastered the basics, experiment with your own individual style. I've written this script using 'my' instead of 'your'. Most people find it easier to control their body if they address it with the personal pronoun. If you prefer, try it the other way round. As for pace, the slower the better. You need time to feel the relaxation flowing into each body part. Try slowing the script down as much as you can without getting bored. The mother voice works well for this exercise; it evokes the soothing 'go to bed' voice used by most mothers for their infants. If there's a certain part of your body that really holds tension (neck? stomach?), switch to the father voice to 'command' it away. Play with your hypnotic voice by stressing certain words. This script uses the word 'relax' or 'relaxation' forty-three times. See if you can discover forty-three different ways to say the word.

You now have enough skills to put yourself through a short self-hypnosis session (without reprogramming). Start with the Finger-Raise Test. Then adjust your breathing with the Relaxed Breathing Script. Then do the Progressive Relaxation Exercise. You'll have to choose whether to use 'my' or 'your', and change one of the scripts accordingly. Spend no more than fifteen minutes on the whole session. Whatever you do, don't get hung up on 'doing it right'. As part of my hypnotherapy session, each client goes into a trance for about thirty minutes. After thousands of trances, I still don't think I ever gave a 'perfect' session where I didn't stumble over a word or make a mistake. As long as hypnosis is based on positive thinking, it will do you no harm. Do your best and call it good.

Setting the Stage

There are two more factors which directly affect how well these focused relaxation exercises – and self-hypnosis – will work for you: mind-set and setting.

Mind-set is the frame of mind you're in when you hypnotise yourself. If you're calm and relaxed when you start your self-hypnosis, you'll sink quickly and deeply into trance. If you're tense and stressed, it will be much more difficult to attain trance depth. This presents something of a problem. Like meditation, self-hypnosis is a way to *stop* tension and stress. So, in some ways, the best time to practise self-hypnosis is when you're wound up. It provides immediate stress relief. Use it as a stress reliever often and early enough and you'll eventually train yourself automatically to 'switch off' stress. On the other hand, you're probably looking to change a mental or physical habit, not just relieve stress. The best time to make a subconscious change is when your mind is free from everyday worries or tensions. It's a trade-off. Either mind-set is acceptable, as long as you recognise the advantages and disadvantages of each.

Ideally, you should *choose* your mind-set. The easiest way to do this is to decide when you're going to practise. There is no perfect time to do self-hypnosis. It depends entirely on your personal schedule and psychology. A mother with young children usually hits the ground running in the morning and doesn't stop all day (although she probably should). She may want to wake up fifteen minutes earlier to do her daily self-hypnosis. Or she may not. If she's the type of woman who desperately needs her sleep, or can't get her motor running before that first cup of coffee, pre-kiddie wake-up self-hypnosis would be a bad idea. If, however, she's always loved the early morning peace of a sleeping family, it would be a perfect time to explore her inner world. Only you know what quiet time you can make available for self-hypnosis, and how you're likely to feel at that moment.

Try and choose a time when you don't have pressing concerns. It's hard to relax if you're thinking about calls to make, food to cook, children to collect, etc. Also, practise at a time of day when you're unlikely to be interrupted or distracted. Nothing harmful or damaging will happen if someone breaks your trance. You'll just wake up and deal with the situation, in the same way you'd wake up out of a deep sleep if you smelled smoke or heard your child crying. Even so, a good self-hypnosis session is like a good film: it has a beginning, middle and end. Unnecessary interruptions ruin your concentration and lower your pleasure. Finally, choose a time when you're awake and alert. Unless you're using self-hypnosis to cure insomnia, you don't want to drift off to sleep in the middle of a trance. It's very pleasant to go from trance to sleep, but sleep is completely ineffective for subconscious modification.

Setting is the place where you practise self-hypnosis. Your environment has an enormous impact on your ability to achieve a deep, life-changing trance. If you're trying to practise self-hypnosis in the terraces of a football stadium or in the middle of a family dinner, good luck. You'll get far better hypnotic results if you put yourself in trance while lying on a beautiful white sandy beach. Or resting in a comfortable deck chair high atop a Swiss Alp. Of course, the indoor type would get better trance results if he or she sat in front of a wood fire in a mountain cabin. Or sitting propped up with pillows on Grandma's comfy sofa. If you visited these types of settings daily and the conditions were consistently perfect, you might be so relaxed you wouldn't *need* hypnosis. Most of us have to make do with a lot less. We have to find or make a place for self-hypnosis that shares as many of the characteristics of these beauty spots as possible.

For example, the beach and the cabin scenarios are telephone-free. There's nothing more trance-disturbing than a ringing telephone – unless it's the sound of your baby crying. Or someone arguing. Self-hypnosis is best practised in a place where there are no noises to distract you. (They don't call it peace *and* quiet for nothing.) At the very least, find the quietest spot possible, close the door and unplug the phones. Even that may not be enough. In a familiar environment, every noise means something. The post hits the mat and the next thing you know you're wondering if you remembered to pay the gas bill. Luckily, this problem tends to go away with practice. But if you can't shut out or ignore distracting sounds, block them out with a music or effects tape (played through headphones, if possible). The best tapes are either sound-effects such as a beach or forest, or spacey New Age music.

The setting for your self-hypnosis should also be attractive. The bathroom is a quiet, telephone-free environment, but tiles that need a wash are not a relaxing sight. Find the most attractive yet quiet place for your self-hypnosis, and face the most pleasing view. If your home or office isn't inspirational, a poster or painting of a beautiful scene should do the trick. While settling in for your self-hypnosis, contemplate the view or image to get yourself psychologically prepared. You can also beautify your setting with hypnotic aromas. For centuries, organised religions have burned exotic oils to help induce a meditative state. A healthfood store or specialist aromatherapy supplier will advise you on which joss sticks or essential oils will help you to achieve greater trance depth. (Remember: unless you're using hypnosis for sleep, you want a scent to help you concentrate.)

To create a perfect blend of mind-set and setting, establish your own pre-hypnosis ritual. Shut the door, unplug the phone, loosen your clothing, get really comfortable, look at something pleasing, think about what you're going to do, start your music tape (if you decide to use one), then close your eyes. Get yourself prepared for self-hypnosis in the same way, at the same time, each and every day. Just as you start feeling hungry around mealtime, your pre-trance ritual will train your subconscious to feel more peaceful and receptive as trance time approaches. The ritual will set the stage for the drama to follow.

14

Down to Perfect Peace

You now have all the skills you need to practise self-hypnosis. By closing your eyes, regulating your breathing and inducing progressive relaxation, you will achieve anything from a light to a deep trance. How will you know how deep you've gone? You won't. The only way to measure trance depth is to test. If you're really concerned, skip ahead to Chapter Seventeen, and try some of the advanced tests. It's worth pointing out again that trance depth is not the be-all and end-all of hypnosis. I've seen dozens of cases where hypnotically 'difficult' clients achieved life-changing results. At this stage, it's better to enjoy the wonderful relaxation that you can create than judge yourself against some pre-determined idea of 'how it should feel'. Anyway, why worry about trance depth before learning how to create it? It's easy to sink deeper and deeper into a deeper and deeper trance. All you have to do is use your imagination.

The Staircase

The most common trance-deepening technique is to imagine walking down a set of stairs. Imagine yourself going down a staircase and your subconscious mind will shift gears and become more receptive to new programming. It's not clear why this technique works so well.

Perhaps your subconscious was trained from childhood to think of going down stairs as a change in consciousness. When you're an infant, stairs separate different worlds. Going down stairs meant changing realities – from 'up here' to 'down there'. An imaginary stair descent may also relax the mind because going down stairs in real life requires both conscious and subconscious control. Both parts of your mind are linked by a common task; the subconscious and conscious mind are focused but relaxed by this partnership. In any case, you don't need to know why this technique is successful to put it to work for you. Give it a try. If you feel more relaxed at the end than at the start, you're doing fine.

Begin by memorising this script, or at least reading it enough times so you can remember the basics:

> I am standing at the top of a beautiful staircase. A safe, wide staircase. The staircase has twenty stairs. Twenty stairs down. Down to perfect peace. Down to total relaxation.
>
> In a moment's time, I will count down from twenty. As I count down, I will take one step down. One step down. With each number down. Feeling more and more relaxed. With each stair down.
>
> When I reach the bottom of the stairs . . . When I reach the number one . . . I will be perfectly relaxed. Wonderfully comfortable. And deeply hypnotised.
>
> Twenty. Nineteen. Eighteen. Seventeen. Sixteen. Fifteen. Fourteen. Thirteen. Twelve. Eleven. Ten. Nine. Eight. Seven. Six. Five. Four. Three. Two. One.
>
> Deeper and deeper. Deeper and deeper. Relaxed and calm. With each breath out, I feel more and more relaxed.

Settle into your quiet and comfortable place. Say the word 'sleep' out loud, tug one ear lobe and close your eyes. Tugging your ear lobe is an 'anchoring technique', linking a relaxed state of mind to your ear lobe. (It can also create instant trance as an associating post-hypnotic suggestion. See Chapter Seventeen). Take a couple of minutes to concentrate on, control and relax your breathing. If you're feeling particularly tense – or simply enjoy the feeling – do the progressive relaxation exercise. Otherwise, imagine a staircase. Really take the time to 'see' the staircase. Is it wood or metal? Carpeted or bare? Where are the hand rails? Imagining a real staircase certainly helps, but don't imagine a staircase that you associate with a stressful environment. When you're focused and relaxed, use the stair script. When you're at the bottom of the stairs, spend a minute or so breathing quietly. Then count to five out loud, open your eyes, stretch and smile.

Advanced Stair Exercise

By now, you've probably settled on a comfortable combination of hypnotic voice, pace and suggestion. Don't! Continue experimenting with your personal style. To increase the effectiveness of the staircase technique, pay special attention to the connection between your breathing and your pacing. Make sure your breathing is nice and easy and slow during the first part of the script. Then, when counting down, say each number at the end of each breath out. This may seem a small innovation, but it isn't. It will have a profound effect on your trance depth.

Try finishing each sentence on the out breath. In other words, remain silent as you draw air in. Then say your script as you let the breath out. Relax on the breath in. Instruct on the breath out. You may have to break up sentences into abnormal sounding bits, but the strange pauses will seem less strange over time. The results are worth it.

Your Special Place

With all this talk about trance depth, you may be wondering where you're supposed to be going down *to*. Because every person experiences trance a little differently, there's no one answer to that question. That said, there are certain mental and physical symptoms which are fairly common to the trance state. For example, most people experience some form of sensory distortion. During these exercises, you may have felt that your hands or feet seemed really large, like huge blocks of cement. You may also have experienced temporal displacement; you awake to find that hardly any time has gone by. And most important for trance depth, you may have begun to realise there is no *where* in trance. Time, space and distance mean nothing in trance. You could be anywhere, or nowhere at all. When you're sinking into a deep trance, you are going down to . . . anywhere you like.

To change your life, this is where you're going: the most beautiful, calm and relaxing place you can possibly imagine. You're going down to your special place. It can be any place at all – some place you've been before or some place entirely in your imagination. It must be safe. You don't want anyone or anything disturbing your peace of mind when you're there. If it's some place you've been before, it must be some place you associate with happy memories. It must be some place vivid. You must be able to recall or imagine it in every detail: sight, sound, smell, taste and feel. It must be some place deeply peaceful. Special places in 'the real world' are spiritually calming; the same should be true for your imaginary special place.

Popular special places include lying on a beach, snuggling up in bed, looking out over mountains, floating in the clouds, resting in a forest glade, warming beside a log fire, swinging in a hammock and drifting under the sea. Feel free to choose any place at all which appeals to you, whether it's as commonplace as your front lounge or as fantastic as a magic castle. Choose your special place now. You can always change your special place, *but not while you're in trance*. Skipping around from place to place in trance wears you out and ruins your concentration. If you choose a place now, only to discover that it's not all that clear or relaxing in trance, stick with your choice anyway. There are going to be days when self-hypnosis is easy, and days when it's going to be difficult. Your special place is not likely to be the thing that decides how well you're able to focus and relax. However, it is the thing which will *keep* you focused and relaxed.

After you've chosen you're special place, tug your ear lobe, say the word 'sleep' out loud and close your eyes. Control your breathing, then go down the stairs. Then repeat the following script:

> I am now in my special place. It is the most safe, warm and comfortable place I can imagine. I am safe, warm and comfortable. There is no where to go and nothing to do. I am relaxing in my special place.

Spend about thirty seconds hypnotising yourself into deeper relaxation, using the above script as a guide. (As long as you use the word 'relax' somewhere in the sentence, you can't go wrong.) Then enjoy your special place in any way you like – walk, run, swim, ride, fly, whatever. The only rule is that *you must stay in your special place, no matter where your thoughts may try to take you.* To avoid drifting off, be active in your special place. If you just imagine lying on a beach soaking up the rays, you're far more likely to drift mentally than if you take an imaginary walk by the water's edge. Should staying in your special place become a real problem, in the next session change your special place to somewhere a little more interesting and a little less relaxing. After about five minutes, use the following 'wake-up script' with a lively and enthusiastic hypnotic voice.

Wake-Up Script

> In a moment's time, I'll count to five. On the number five, I'll wake up feeling refreshed and relaxed, like I've had a long and peaceful sleep.

One   *I feel refreshed and relaxed, like I've had a long and peaceful sleep.*
Two   *I feel mentally and physically balanced.*
Three *I feel mentally and physically balanced and perfect. Perfect in every way.*
Four *Energy flowing into my mind and body now. My body is rested. My thoughts are sharp and clear.*
Five *I am awake and alert. I'm ready for anything.*

Special Place Deepening Technique

To immerse yourself in your special place, to let the peace and relaxation of your special place flow through your mind and body, you need to focus your mind intensely. You need to concentrate on each of your five senses, one by one. Start with sight. When you're in your special place, say the following:

> Everything I see is what I would see in my special place. And everything I see is relaxing me deeper.

Then use your imagination to see something really beautiful and relaxing in your special place. It could be a flower, the sea sparkling in the sunshine or a beautiful mountain vista. *When you can see or imagine something beautiful and relaxing, raise one of your fingers.*
  To deepen the trance even further, say:

> The higher up my finger raises, the more relaxed I feel.

Let your finger rise up. Then say:

> When I drop my finger, I will sink deeper into trance.

Then drop your finger and feel the trance deepen.
After a long pause, move on to the next sense:

> Everything I hear is what I would hear in my special place. And everything I hear is relaxing me deeper.

When you can hear or imagine hearing something beautiful and relaxing, raise one of your fingers. To deepen the trance even further, say:

> The higher up my finger raises, the more relaxed I feel.

Let your finger rise up. Then say:

> When I drop my finger, I will sink deeper into trance.

Then drop your finger and feel the trance deepen. Repeat the technique for your sense of touch, taste and smell. As everyone has a particular sense that they favour (usually sight or sound), some senses will probably take longer than others. Don't be impatient. I've had clients who needed more than two minutes before they could imagine a beautiful smell associated with their special place. Always remember that self-hypnosis is more a skill than a talent.
  Some people get very concerned that they don't 'really' see, smell, touch, taste or hear something in their special place. David Soskis, author of *Teaching Self-Hypnosis*, defines hypnosis as 'a process that allows us to experience thoughts and images as real'. Great, but what is real? At the end of the day, reality is what you think it is. So if you can get even a vague idea of your senses within your special place – if you kind of know what it *might* be like to see, hear, etc. something in your special place – you've achieved the goal. Obviously, you're not

really *there*, in your special place. Anyone watching you would swear on a stack of Bibles that you never left your chair or bed. But another more profound sense, you *are* somewhere peaceful and safe and relaxing. The distinction is not really important. Trance should be something you feel, not analyse. Don't let intellectual considerations destroy the experience.

Repetition Rules!

The imaginary flight of stairs is the old faithful of self-hypnosis. A lot of hypnotists feel it's too boring and look for something more creative. They play with variations on the theme, including a lift (count down twenty floors), an escalator (count down from twenty as you descend), or ladder (count the rungs). The brave go for things like an imaginary parachute jump or a downhill ski-run. At the end of the day, anything that takes down in your imagination will work. Although you're free to experiment, beginning self-hypnotists are well advised to stay with the stair technique for at least the first twenty trances. There's a lot for your subconscious to work on without presenting it with new deepening techniques. In fact, a predictable routine is itself the best deepening technique. Keep your self-hypnosis simple and predictable, and every time you go down into trance, you'll go down a little deeper.

The golden rule of self-hypnosis is: 'Just do it.' Despite my careful step-by-step instructions, it really doesn't matter how, how well, where or when you do your self-hypnosis, as long as you do it. Nothing is more important to attaining deep trance than sheer persistence. Forget talent. Forget your burning desire to solve your problem right this second. If you stay with self-hypnosis long enough, you will attain deep trance. You will change your subconscious programmes. You will eliminate bad habits, ease your mind, grow larger breasts or whatever else you're seeking. So don't envy anyone their hypnotic talents. Kick back and relax.

15

Affirmations

When we talk to someone, we speak conscious mind to conscious mind. We discuss or debate facts, share experiences, make plans and generally operate on a rational level. At the same time, we hold a subconscious conversation. We exchange hidden messages through gesture, tone of voice, body language, eye contact and other non-verbal signals. We rarely make a conscious effort to respond to this subconscious feedback. But what if you *did* want to change someone else's subconscious responses: their breathing, posture and facial expressions? Altering your conversation – being highly supportive or aggressive – would work. But the best solution would be to communicate on the subconscious level by changing *your* tone of voice, posture and eye contact. As for your words, you'd need to really understand how the subconscious mind works. You'd need to speak a different language.

For self-hypnosis to work, you need to overcome the subconscious–conscious language barrier. The inner mind thinks. The subconscious mind reacts. The inner mind reasons. The subconscious mind responds. You can't expect your inner mind to change deeply ingrained habits simply because your conscious mind gives the subconscious all the rational arguments for change. If the subconscious worked that way, you could get everyone to stop smoking by showing them cancer mortality figures and a picture of a diseased lung. As you know, that approach doesn't work. The subconscious has its own way of doing things. Once you know how it works, once you know how to communicate effectively, it's relatively easy to convince your subconscious mind to do things that will benefit 'both' of you.

There are many ways to think about your inner mind. Again, one of the most popular is to think of your subconscious as a five-year-old child. Like most five-year-olds, it's a little slow. Speak to it slowly and clearly, and it just about understands what you're getting at. The subconscious mind is very emotional. Love it, and it feels safe and secure. Criticise it, and it lacks confidence. Your inner mind depends entirely on you (the rational adult) for its understanding of how the world works.

How well are your communicating with your inner mind right now? All your conscious thoughts are messages to your inner mind. What happens if you judge your thoughts against the needs of your inner mind? The subconscious mind has limited intellectual ability and a short attention span. New ideas have to be presented very simply and powerfully. Are you analysing your problems in such detail that your inner mind is paralysed by confusion? The subconscious mind needs constant support and encouragement. Are you criticizing yourself so much that your inner mind feels weak and stupid? The subconscious mind always tries to do what you want it to do. When did you last tell your inner mind exactly what you want it to do?

Here's your chance. To change your life, get yourself down into your deepest trance and talk to your subconscious mind. Your hypnotic 'conversation' is actually the repetition of a single sentence called an *affirmation*. An affirmation is a simple, short and totally positive statement in the present tense. It's a new and improved subconscious programme, carefully designed to replace faulty subconscious habits or ideas, or trigger natural physical reactions. For example, many people have a subconscious stimulus–response pattern that makes them tense or nervous in a certain situation. Once they're hypnotised, they can use the affirmation, 'I am calm, confident and relaxed in every situation' to change their response to the negative stimulus. Implanted deeply enough, the affirmation will replace the old stress programme with a new, relaxed programme.

Don't be fooled by the simplicity of the affirmation concept. Repeated five times in daily self-hypnosis, a single positive affirmation can create a miraculous change in thought, emotion, behaviour and health.

To modify subconscious programmes, you need the right affirmation. A general affirmation like the one above can do no harm, but it's not half as effective as an affirmation targeted on a short-term goal. If you want to be calm, confident and relaxed in *every* situation, start with being calm, confident and relaxed in *one* situation. Success breeds success; you see the change and build from there. Only you know what change is desirable, and measurable. Let's say you're a business person who wants to sell a product to potential customers. Your affirmation could be, 'I am calm, confident and relaxed whenever I meet potential customers.' Is that enough? Maybe. Maybe relaxation isn't the key to what you *really* want: sales. Perhaps your affirmation should be, 'I explain the benefits of my product easily, effortlessly and automatically' or 'New clients love to do business with me.' Affirmations are not as easy as they first appear.

To create a powerful affirmation, understand that the subconscious always says 'yes'. No matter what question you ask, the answer is *always* yes. So why doesn't your inner mind say 'yes' to bungee jumping? It does! It says 'yes' to staying alive. The conscious mind then translates this 'yes' response into the word 'no'. The subconscious mind is a world of competing 'yes' responses. That's why you can't get your inner mind to say 'No!' to a chocolate bar, cigarette, stress reaction, etc. All you can do is cajole, inspire, bribe and/or train your inner mind to say 'yes' to something better: being slim, breathing fresh clean air, or remaining relaxed under pressure. A positive affirmation such as, 'I eat the perfect amount of ice cream', 'I enjoy breathing fresh, clean air' or 'I am perfectly calm at parties' inspires your subconscious mind to say 'yes!' to change.

Other than simplicity, all effective affirmations have immediacy. The inner mind doesn't have a firm grasp on the concept of time (one reason why time distorts in trance). It can't make subtle distinctions between the past, present or future. Powerful affirmations exploit this limitation by presenting change as a done deal, a *fait accompli*. By using the present tense – I *am* a non-smoker rather than I *will be* a non-smoker – you convince your inner mind that change has *already happened*. This deception relaxes the inner mind (there's nothing to worry about) and gets it to 'continue doing' what it thinks it's already doing. Remember: the inner mind is literal-minded. If you say I *will* be a non-smoker, it thinks great, there's no rush. If you say I *want to be* a non-smoker, it still thinks great, there's no rush. If you say I *am* a non-smoker, it thinks, *hmmm*, if I'm a non-smoker, I should stop smoking.

Instructions

Once you've chosen your affirmation, put yourself into a trance, use a deepening technique (or two) and enter your special place. Spend a few minutes enjoying your special place. Then find somewhere comfortable to rest, get mentally settled in, and repeat your affirmation five times *slowly*. Your affirmation is the main event. It's the reason you've put yourself into a trance. So say it with gusto and determination. Say your affirmation with faith, as if there's no doubt in your mind whatsoever that you have already achieved your goal. Then use the wake-up script (see page 125) to come out of trance.

You will soon learn to add the last ingredient – creative visualisation – to the mix. For now, know this: there is nothing in the world stronger than a positive thought properly presented to your inner mind. Nothing.

What's Your Affirmation?

The following section offers guidance on a problem-by-problem basis. Take the time now to go back to Chapter Ten and refresh your memory about your strategy for change. Your affirmation should be crafted within that framework.

Giving Up Smoking

I'm not a big fan of going cold turkey. Clients who say, 'That's it, that's my last cigarette' are setting themselves up for failure. When you go cold turkey, you're never more than one cigarette away from total failure. You light up, then you give up giving up. But if you gradually cut down on your smoking, you're only one cigarette away from success. Every cigarette you *don't* smoke is one cigarette closer to stopping. Review your list of every cigarette you smoke and the 'extra' ones with the star next to them. These are the cigarettes that will start you on the road to breathing fresh clean air. These are the cigarettes you want to eliminate through your affirmation. Target a specific smoking programme (i.e., a time and place you normally smoke) and create an affirmation to counter it.

Don't use the word 'don't'! For example, to eliminate a 'stuck in traffic' cigarette, the worst possible affirmation is: 'I don't smoke in traffic'. As your subconscious doesn't understand the word 'don't', that affirmation would reinforce the habit! (If I say 'don't think of a pink elephant', what's the first think you think about?) There are many creative ways around this problem. You could focus your affirmation on your hands: 'My hands rest comfortably on the steering wheel in traffic'. You could distract yourself: 'I concentrate intensely on the radio when I'm in traffic'. You could flood your mind with relaxation: 'I am totally relaxed and calm in traffic'. Think about why you smoke in traffic, then counter the impulse with pinpointed positive thinking.

Cigarette smoking is really a collection of smoking programmes. Once you've stopped the 'extra' cigarettes, you'll have to move on to the more pleasurable cigarettes. These will be harder to shift. They will require more creative, personal and powerful affirmations. Hopefully, by this point, you'll have confidence in self-hypnosis and your ability to control your own habits. Whatever does or does not

happen, stick with it. If an affirmation isn't working after five to seven
sessions, try another. And another. Don't rush. Breathing fresh clean air
is one of the most important things you can do for your health and happiness. As long as you use the five rules of writing affirmations (page
154) and practise daily self-hypnosis, you will eventually get there.

One important thing to keep in mind is that your self-hypnosis may
not entirely eliminate the urge to smoke. I believe that contrary to current thinking, an urge to smoke is not a physical craving for nicotine.
An urge to smoke is a thought that creates a physical craving for nicotine.
These thoughts are habitual. You sit down in front of the TV and you
get a habitual thought that now's the time to smoke. Like all habits,
these smoking thoughts will go away with time, as long as you don't
indulge them. Have you ever moved house or slept in a hotel room on
holiday, woken up in the middle of the night and gone the wrong way
towards the toilet? Eventually, the confusion went away as you re-
trained your subconscious mind. Eventually, your urges to smoke will
go away. Every time you resist the thought to smoke, the urge dimin-
ishes. Old habits may die hard (they may also die easy), but die they do.

Once you've cut down your cigarettes to a certain level, you're
going to be faced with the decision to quit entirely. First, make sure
you're ready. If you're not ready to surrender those last few cigarettes,
don't. Do some more thinking about how your life will be better without cigarettes. Re-write your lists of positives and negatives. At the
same time, keep practising your self-hypnosis. When you are ready,
switch to a more general affirmation. This new programme will convince your inner mind to let go completely. For example, you can use:
'I enjoy breathing fresh, clean air' or 'I enjoy all the benefits of being a
non-smoker'. Your list of positives can help you find the right inspiration: 'I love raising my kids as a non-smoker' or 'I exercise regularly,
with clean, healthy lungs'.

The decision to quit smoking is a big decision, but don't make it a
big deal. If you quit, then start again, quit again. Keep quitting until
you quit for good. Stay with your daily self-hypnosis for at least two
weeks after your last cigarette. If you feel the old smoking urge
months later, go back to your self-hypnosis and root it out. Lots of
people have used hypnosis to stop smoking for good. You can too.

Staying Slim and Feeling Healthy

Healthy eating hypnosis should start with a general affirmation and
move towards the specific. Some people try to lose weight or stop eat-

ing disorders by focusing on a particular problem food. They think that if they could just stop eating chocolate or bread or biscuits, they'd be in total control of their weight. Not so. Control over food and eating comes from creating an entire healthy diet; eating enough healthy food to make sensible choices. If you use self-hypnosis to try to control a specific food before establishing a healthy-eating framework, you'll be making the problem worse. You will be too hungry to resist your problem food. Even worse, you'll be creating a food obsession. The more you concentrate on eliminating a given food, the more you're thinking about it. The more you think about it, the harder it is *not* to think about it.

A general affirmation calms you down and sets you off in the right direction. The HypnoHealth eating plan is an effective, all-encompassing affirmation: 'I eat small amounts of healthy food throughout the day to keep hunger away' or 'I am naturally attracted to small amounts of healthy food throughout the day'. For those who don't need to sell the healthy eating concept to their inner mind, something slightly more inspirational can work wonders. 'I am losing weight easily, effortlessly and automatically' has proven itself countless times. People with eating disorders should not use weight-loss affirmations, or try anything too intellectual. 'I have a positive relationship with food independent of my mother's needs' is not as good as 'I enjoy eating normally'.

Stick with your general affirmation for at least seven days of full self-hypnosis. After you've established a healthy eating pattern, you can begin to isolate what eating or exercise habits stand between you and your goal. Single-out a particular problem area and think about what positive thought could banish it from your life. The exact affirmation that will make the change depends on your challenge and personal psychology. For example, if you're snacking excessively after dinner, your affirmation can be: 'The later it gets, the more satisfied I feel' or 'I eat just enough dinner to last until breakfast'. For people who have trouble getting down to exercise, a specific affirmation such as: 'I feel relaxed and happy riding the exercise bike' or 'I love moving my body in aerobics class' can substantially increase motivation.

While addressing these challenges one by one, try to keep things in perspective. Don't be a perfectionist. As long as the trend is in the right direction, you don't need to eliminate all your bad habits. You just need patience. Use your affirmation to give your inner mind some new directions, then give it the time and space it needs to get on with the job.

Conquering a Phobia

Phobias tend to be very specific. People who are afraid of flying aren't usually phobic of spiders, and people who are afraid of open spaces aren't usually phobic of street crime. On one hand, the fact that your fear is focused on one specific stimulus creates a stronger than normal subconscious reaction. On the other hand, your focused fear makes it easy to create a powerful affirmation. You can easily identify the exact programme making you miserable and devise an effective affirmation to counter it. Be specific, be positive (don't use an affirmation starting with 'I am not afraid of . . .'), and you can't go far wrong. An affirmation like 'I feel wonderfully calm and relaxed around spiders' or 'I love the freedom of wide-open spaces' can be all you need to change a lifetime phobia.

If your phobic response is very strong, you may not be comfortable with affirmations like the ones above. In that case, you need to break the problem down and tackle each subconscious response one at a time. If you've done the phobia groundwork described in Chapter Ten, you know how, what, when and where you react to the negative stimulus. Choose one part of your subconscious reaction and design an affirmation to stop it. For example, imagine a young boy who is petrified of girls. Whenever he tries to talk to a girl, his hands go clammy, his stomach ties up in knots and he stammers terribly. An affirmation such as 'My hands stay dry and comfortable whenever I talk to a girl' can be better than 'I love talking to girls'. When the boy discovers that he can control the temperature of his hands in this stressful situation, both his conscious and subconscious mind feel more confident about tackling the next symptom. And the next.

Hypnotherapists love phobias because they're relatively easy to identify and cure. As a self-hypnotist, get ready for a treat. It may take a while, but once you cure your phobia you'll feel a rush of self-confidence. Don't forget where this confidence comes from, so that you continue to respect and enjoy your inner mind.

Building Up Confidence and Self-Esteem

A perfect affirmation for people with low self-esteem, is, 'I feel calm, confident and relaxed in every situation'. This can create the subconscious changes you need to build confidence in your inner self. It can be the positive thought that takes you from self-loathing to self-loving.

However, this general affirmation requires a huge leap of faith – a belief that you will get all the way from here (feelings of worthlessness) to there (total confidence). It takes a lot of self-hypnosis to convince your subconscious that it can achieve this long-term goal. A lack of perceived success *en route* could mean a loss of faith and a journey back into the abyss. So, rather than conjuring an inspirational vision of the whole building of your new, confident self, your first affirmation can lay the foundations.

Your first ego-enhancing affirmation should be goal-directed. It must be targeted at a particular situation where you feel a lack of confidence (the stimulus), and the physical or emotional symptoms triggered in these situations (the response). Take a piece of paper and write down one situation where you feel inadequate. Be specific. For example, 'At parties where I don't know more than two or three people' or 'At work when I see others laughing and joking'. Then list your reactions: nervousness, depression, can't speak properly, funny tummy, crankiness, etc. Your affirmation should address both the situation and the response in totally positive terms. For example, 'My stomach feels wonderfully calm at large parties' or 'I am totally confident of my abilities at work when other people are feeling tense'.

Depending on your confidence levels, it may be too much to ask to feel good about yourself in a highly pressurised situation. When the stakes are high, the possibility of failure can block the relaxation you need to build confidence. In that case, your first affirmation should be directed at a situation where there is nothing to lose. 'I feel masterful when making tea' is not as silly as it sounds. When you feel a change in your self-awareness during tea-making, you gain confidence in your ability to feel confident. You can then apply your hypnotic technique to something a bit more ambitious. Just as a baby learns to crawl before it learns to walk, you may need to feel calm in private before you can feel satisfied with yourself in public.

Curing Insomnia

Nothing could be simpler than a sleep affirmation – provided you've taken down the barriers to a good night's sleep. If you find you can't cut down or eliminate alcohol, late-night red meat, over-work, worry, etc., you'll first need an affirmation that changes these insomnia-producing habits. 'I enjoy drinking fresh, clean mineral water', 'I love eating delicious light foods for dinner', 'My free time is even more important and enjoyable than my work' and 'I enjoy thinking about positive people, places and events' are all affirmations working in the direction of healthy, uninterrupted sleep. Once you have modified the worst of these sleep-preventers, you can then expect to get fantastic results from the simple affirmation, 'I sleep peacefully and awake refreshed'.

I definitely recommend that people who have trouble sleeping practise self-hypnosis when they're *not* sleeping. As I've said many times before, to reprogramme your subconscious mind successfully you must be awake and alert. Realistically, I know that the vast majority of people who buy *HypnoHealth* to overcome insomnia are going to use self-hypnosis at bedtime to get to sleep. Fair enough. It's not that hard to slip from the hypnotic state to the sleep state. Do it often enough and you will be able to slip quietly into the land of dreams without hypnosis. For those who want to take this approach, this is the end of the line. Your entire self-hypnosis routine is:

1. Put yourself into a trance.
2. Use the progressive relaxation, stairs and advanced special place deepening techniques.
3. Actively enjoy your special place until you're mentally tired.
4. Find some place comfortable in your special place to lie down.
5. Repeat the affirmation 'I am sleeping peacefully' over and over.
6. Sleep.

Don't worry if this approach doesn't work straightaway. If you don't drift off to sleep, stay *in your special place*. Go off and enjoy an imaginary exploration, exercise, conversation, whatever you like. Concentrate hard on the events in your special place so you will mentally exhaust yourself. Then try settling down in your comfortable spot again and repeating your affirmation. No matter what happens, it's a no-lose situation. Even if it takes you ages to get to sleep, even if you don't get to sleep at all, you will at least rest comfortably in a hypnotic state. Your mind and body will have taken a break from everyday stress. You will enjoy all the benefits of total relaxation.

Breast Enhancement

Creating a powerful breast-enhancement affirmation couldn't be easier. Decide exactly what size you'd like your breasts to be, then write an affirmation to pass the message to your subconscious mind. For example, 'I have perfect 34C breasts'. If you like, you can add a couple of inspirational adjectives, such as 'I have perfectly shaped, 34C breasts' or 'I have large, firm, 34C breasts'. The other approach worth considering is the equally simple, 'My breasts are growing larger'. Once again, feel free to be more specific and inspirational, such as 'My breasts are growing larger and firmer' or 'My breasts are growing larger and more beautiful every day, in every way'. Once you decide on the best affirmation for you, stay with it.

Women seeking hypnotic breast enhancement need to practise their self-hypnosis a little differently from people facing other challenges. First of all, it's worth repeating that growth requires at least two months of daily self-hypnosis. Equally important, you need to modify the self-hypnosis routine slightly. When you get comfortable in your special place – *before you say your affirmation* – warm your breasts hypnotically. There are many ways to do this. If your special place is somewhere warm like a beach, imagine lying topless in a blazing hot sun. (If necessary, you can switch your special place at this point.) You can also imagine taking a really hot shower and letting the hot water spray on to your breasts. Other warming images include a hair dryer, hot towels, a sauna and a massage with warm oils. Use whatever imaginary sensations work for you.

Under hypnosis, the breast-warming imagery will trick your subconscious into sending extra blood flowing into your breasts (to cool them down). As explained earlier, this expands the blood vessels and helps create the growth. (Even if that theory isn't valid, the hypnotic warming focuses your subconscious mind on your breasts in a pleasant way.) To maximise the effect, make sure you practise your self-hypnosis somewhere warm. Also, command the sensation to increase with this script:

> I'm going to count to five. My breasts will grow warmer and warmer with each number. By the time I reach the number five, they will be very, very hot. One. Warmer and warmer. Two. Warmer and warmer. Three. Warmer and warmer. Four. Really hot now. Five. My breasts are very, very hot.

Like all aspects of self-hypnosis, hypnotic breast warming improves with practice. It's often helpful to put yourself into a trance when you're experiencing something warm on your chest and hypnotically 'capture' the feeling. All you do is tug your ear lobe and say sleep, imagine going down the stairs, then say:

> Whenever I want to re-create this feeling of warmth in my breasts, I will simply rub my ear lobe when I'm in trance.

Rub your ear lobe for a minute, then use the wake-up script. If you use this capture technique, when you practise your self-hypnosis, rub your ear lobe when you're imagining the warming sensation.

After you've warmed your breasts, say your affirmation five times slowly. Proceed to the creative visualisation explained in the next chapter. Another technique which can improve results is to leave your breasts hypnotised. Alter the wake-up script slightly, saying:

> I will awake on the number five feeling refreshed and relaxed, like I've had a long and peaceful sleep. I will leave my breasts in trance, feeling warm and relaxed. These sensations will continue as a signal to my inner mind to continue the process of growth even after I come out of a trance. One. Etc.

Whether or not you leave your breasts hypnotised, make sure you wake up feeling good about your body – the way it is and the way it will be.

Overcoming Stress

The antidote to stress is relaxation. Just as a general antibiotic can kill a specific virus, a general affirmation can relieve a specific stress reaction. An all-encompassing relaxation affirmation can create a feeling of well-being, safety and security that no person or event can disturb. The affirmation 'I am perfectly calm and relaxed in all situations' can stop you from being stressed in traffic jams or bank queues. As you are experiencing perfect calm and relaxation in your trance state, your inner mind knows what you expect from it later. Also, since your inner mind enjoys this feeling of trance, it's receptive to the idea of re-creating this feeling in response to a specific stimulus. A general anti-stress affirmation like 'Every day in every way, I am feeling more and more relaxed' will create a bridge from trance relaxation to non-trance relaxation, improving your life in many, many ways.

Even so, a general affirmation will never be as powerful as an affirmation specifically targeted at your specific stress creator. A sensible affirmation zeroes-in on the precise problem that needs fixing. It also creates a sense of mastery that will, in itself, reduce your stress levels. When you feel in control of a situation, you don't get worked up – even if it doesn't go exactly as planned. Review your list of what, when, where, who and how you get stressed. Then create an affirmation that deals directly with the stress trigger. 'I am perfectly calm and relaxed with my mother-in-law' or 'I love giving Thursday sales presentations' tells your inner mind in no uncertain terms what it has to do.

You can also come at the problem from the other direction: your subconscious stress reactions. You can devise an affirmation that alleviates a physical symptom: 'My shoulders relax completely when I talk to suppliers'. You can devise an affirmation to relieve an emotional symptom: 'I feel happy and calm when my children are being difficult'. You can devise an affirmation to interrupt the normal stress sequence: 'The more pressure I'm under, the more relaxed I feel'. You can change a negative coping habit like drinking alcohol into a more positive strategy: 'I let go of all my tension by sitting down with a nice cup of tea'. There is considerable scope for you to come up with your own affirmation which will change or eliminate your subconscious stress programme.

Make sure that your affirmation works towards a measurable goal and measure your achievement. Create a form that rates the success of your subconscious reprogramming. Use it every day. It can be as simple as rating your stress reaction from 1 (none) to 5 (severe):

Goal: to feel less stressed while commuting in morning and evening
Affirmation: 'I feel perfectly relaxed and calm while taking the train to and from work.'

Monday	1	2	3	4	5
Tuesday	1	2	3	4	5
Wednesday	1	2	3	4	5
Thursday	1	2	3	4	5
Friday	1	2	3	4	5

The associative post-hypnotic suggestion (see Chapter Seventeen) is another crucial technique for stress relief. You can use this hypnotic devise to summon trance-like relaxation at the moment of stress. For now, you can rely on any one of the relaxation/self-hypnosis techniques you've learned so far (breathing, stairs, progressive relaxation, special place) as a 'morning-after' pill for stress reactions. After you get stressed, find a quiet place, close your eyes and use one or more of the exercises to soothe your inner mind. Use any technique in any order you choose. For example, you can tug your ear lobe, say 'sleep', and go straight to your special place. Or do a two-minute progressive relaxation. This won't cure your stress reaction, but it will prevent stress from causing long-term damage to your health and happiness.

Stress-reactive exercises are not a substitute for daily self-hypnosis. You want to change these negative stimulus–response habits once and for all. For that, you need to convince your inner mind that there's a better way. There is. Use self-hypnosis to reprogramme yourself to relax in every situation. Living relaxed is the single most important change you can make to improve the quality of your life.

Improving Brain Power

There are two types of affirmations that will increase your brain power: performance or achievement. Performance affirmations unleash the full power of your mental abilities. Like a turbo-charger attached to the engine of your car, these affirmations 'soup-up' your mind's normal abilities. Repeated five times in deep hypnosis, an affirmation like 'My mind soaks up information like a sponge' can literally double your ability to absorb new information. 'I automatically concentrate on whatever I am doing, to the complete exclusion of everything else' or (more simply) 'I concentrate on one thing at a time' can give you the mental focus you need to achieve intellectually challenging tasks. 'My mind is razor-sharp' or 'I can solve any problem, no matter how challenging it appears' will put the power of your inner mind to work on your conscious problems.

While there's nothing wrong with tinkering with your mental engine for maximum performance, you may need to send the car-engine image to the scrap heap. These 'turbo affirmations' are usually not specific enough for a particular challenge. Remember that your inner mind is extremely literal; it does *exactly* what you tell it to do. If you use an affirmation like 'My mind soaks up information like a sponge', you haven't instructed your inner mind about giving *out* information. If you use the affirmation 'My mind is razor-sharp', you consciously know when you want cutting-edge mental ability, but your inner mind may not have a clue. In that sense your inner mind is like a computer: it won't do anything more or less than you tell it to. You need task-specific subconscious re-programming. 'My mind easily absorbs and remembers famous dates in French history' or 'My mind is razor-sharp in business negotiations' are two examples of effective, custom-designed affirmations.

You can also approach brain-power affirmations from the opposite direction: achievement. You work with a wide range of mental abilities: relaxation, concentration, absorption, recall, analysis, comparison, communication, creativity and more. Most intellectual goals require all of these skills. People suffering from exam nerves want to pass their exams. They want to relax in the stressful situation, but they also want to recall and communicate information. People who listen to sophisticated presentations want to absorb details, but they also want to analyse the broader concepts. By implanting an affirmation focusing on the goal – rather than the mental process – you let your inner mind select the abilities it needs to achieve the goal. 'I easily pass all exams and get first-class results' or 'I perform brilliantly at presentations' is specific enough to inspire your inner mind, but general enough that your inner mind can get on with the job at hand.

Experiment with both performance and achievement affirmations to see which works best for you (sticking with one affirmation for a minimum of seven sessions). It may be difficult to tell if your brain-power self-hypnosis is succeeding. Improved exam results and unexpected praise are proof positive that your inner mind is doing its stuff. Unfortunately, this type of independent feedback is usually too rare for you to gain the necessary confidence in your improved abilities. You need to set a specific goal and monitor your achievement. Try and come up with an affirmation that pushes your abilities in measurable ways, such as 'I read and remember ten pages of text' or 'I make a brilliant comment at every sales presentation'. Self-testing is excellent as both practice (to relieve stress and worry) and measurement. Keep the affirmation inspirational, but don't neglect the bottom line.

Relaxation is the key to efficient mental function. As you now know, you are very relaxed in trance. You can learn to trigger trance-like relaxation on demand by mastering the associative post-hypnotic suggestion technique, explained in Chapter Seventeen. Meanwhile, rest assured that simply by going into a daily trance you're training your inner mind to respond to your command. This new partnership between conscious and subconscious mind is already yielding intellectual benefits, whether you know it or not.

Controlling Pain

Pain-control affirmations should always be pain specific. In other words, where does it hurt and how do you want it to feel? 'My shoulder muscles are perfectly relaxed and comfortable' or 'All the joints in my hands are wonderfully supple' tells your inner mind what sensations to create and where to create them. Conjure up the most pleasant and relaxing sensations you can imagine and incorporate them into your affirmation. People who associate warmth with physical comfort should capitalise on that preference: 'My neck muscles are bathed and soothed by perfect warmth' or 'My ribs are coated in a warm, soothing oil'. Appealing to your sense of touch can also be effective: 'My skin is as smooth as silk' or 'My knees are as comfortable as my favourite cashmere jumper'.

Since pain is often a response to specific stimulus, you can use a 'time-released' pain-control affirmation. This type of affirmation

instructs your inner mind to create pleasant sensations when you
need them most. First, identify your pain triggers: time of day, movement, emotional stress, etc. For example, your legs may
hurt when you walk or your skin may feel raw and itchy when you
wake up. Next, use your self-hypnosis to implant a reactive affirmation. Affirmations like 'My legs are warm and relaxed whenever I go
for a walk' or 'Every morning, my skin feels as smooth as a baby's
bottom' will establish a new response to the painful stimulus. The programme will remain dormant until the appropriate moment. At that
moment, the specific situation will automatically trigger the pleasant
feeling. (Since this is a subconscious programme to replace pain, note
that you may not consciously 'feel' the absence of pain.) My ankle used
to throb and go stiff whenever it was cold and wet. I used a time-
released affirmation ('My ankle feels warm and supple whenever it's
cold and wet') to stop this old parachuting wound from giving me
trouble.

Pain elimination requires a different affirmational approach. Once
again, I can't over-emphasise the importance of consulting a medical
professional *before* you attempt this goal. Just because you *can* do
something doesn't mean you *should*. That said, hundreds of thousands
of people are taking enormous doses of chemical painkillers. Hypnotic
pain elimination is far superior. It leaves the immune system intact
and improves mental function.

After your special place, before your affirmation, concentrate hard
on the body part (or parts) that you want to numb. Keep repeating 'My
____ is getting more and more numb. I am feeling less and less sensation in my ____'. At the same time, imagine you're holding cold snow
against that part of your body. Or try to remember when your dentist
made your mouth numb and transfer the feeling to the painful area.
Some people use the memory of when they slept on their arm and
woke up to find it felt like a dead weight. Use whatever imagery or
ideas help create the effect of numbness or lack of sensation. When
you feel sensation diminishing in the affected area, switch your subconscious instruction to 'My ____ is numb. I feel no sensation whatsoever in my ____'.

Keeping your eyes closed, you can test this numbness by gently
pressing a blunt but pointed object (like the top of a pen) into the for-
merly painful area (if applicable). When you're convinced that you've
eliminated sensation in the painful part of your body, say an affirmation that controls this effect: 'My ____ will remain perfectly relaxed
and comfortable (or numb) when I wake up out of trance'. For safety's
sake, give yourself an instant escape hatch: 'My ____ will continue to

feel this way unless I snap my fingers'. For extra safety, some self-hypnotists like to add the instruction, 'If my inner mind knows of any reason why I should feel this pain, it will over-ride these instructions'. Remember that pain-elimination hypnosis is an advanced technique. To eliminate pain completely, you need a very deep trance. To induce a deep trance in self-hypnosis, you need a *lot* of practice.

If you have trouble creating an effective pain-elimination affirmation, or if you want to reduce your pain quickly, try the 'thermostat' technique. In your special place, before your affirmation, imagine a thermostat with a dial reading from one to twenty. Tell yourself: 'This thermostat controls my pain. Twenty is the most pain there is; one is no pain at all.' Take a moment to check the current setting. Since your inner mind controls the setting of the thermostat during hypnosis, you may be surprised to see just how high or low the reading rates your pain. Make a mental note of the setting. Tell yourself, 'As I turn down this dial, my ____ will feel more and more comfortable'. Imagine turning down the dial. Feel your pain diminish. When you're ready, move on to your affirmation, visualisation (see Chapter Sixteen) and wake-up script (see page 125).

Pain is an entirely subjective experience, which means it can't really be measured scientifically. In many ways, it's just as hard to measure on any kind of personal scale. But you *must* make the effort to measure your pain levels. Self-hypnosis often cures or controls pain slowly, bit by bit. Like the advent of Spring, relief can seem to take forever until, one day, it suddenly arrives. Unless you measure your pain and see the improvements, you may not have the discipline to stick with your self-hypnosis. Create a simple form. Every day, note what time you practised your self-hypnosis. Rate your comfort level (*not* pain) on a scale of one to twenty before and after self-hypnosis. Then take a subjective measurement. For example:

MONDAY

Time of self-hypnosis: _____.

Comfort level before self-hypnosis:

1 2 3 4 5 6 7 8 9 10 11 12 13 14 15 16 17 18 19 20

Comfort level after self-hypnosis:

1 2 3 4 5 6 7 8 9 10 11 12 13 14 15 16 17 18 19 20

My pain is:

A) a lot better   B) a bit better   C) about the same
D) a bit worse   E) a lot worse

With practice, self-hypnosis can provide instant pain relief. (Chapter Seventeen will teach you how to learn how to create an instant 'shot' of total relaxation when you're not in trance.) It's a drug-free technique for taking control of your own experience of physical sensation, while increasing the strength of your body's own immune system. Stick with it. Sooner or later, you'll find an inner peace that no physical injury can ever disturb.

Better Sex

What do you like to do in bed? What really turns you on? As long as your sexual excitement doesn't hurt anyone else, you're free to explore the outer limits of desire and pleasure. Or are you? How much experimentation have you tried lately? Until you plant the right affirmation deep inside your subconscious mind, your sexual patterns may be too well fixed for fun. A properly worded affirmation can actually change your sexual personality – what you like and don't like. Once you tap into your inner mind and alter your sexual patterns, you can open an entire world of erotic possibilities. Self-hypnosis can help you find pleasure in sexual activities which you may have dismissed as strange, unacceptable or just plain dull.

Start with a goal. Have a good think about what's currently preventing you from increasing your sexual pleasure. Are you getting enough sex? Are you tired of the same old positions? Are you bored with your lover(s)? Can your mind and body really let go during sex? Do you lack confidence in your own sexual abilities? Do you like your body? Do you like your lover's body? Can you tell your lover exactly what you want him or her to do? Now make a list of exactly what you'd like to change about your sexual habits. (Unless you're non-orgasmic, don't focus too much attention on your orgasms. Most people find that intensifying pre-orgasmic pleasure creates the greatest improvement in sexual satisfaction.) Some of these ideas will lead to personal goals and affirmations, such as 'I love to let go and enjoy sex'. Some goals will require a bit of friendly discussion and negotiation – especially if you're in a long-term relationship. It's no good using an affirmation like 'I enjoy telling my lover how to give me a powerful orgasm' if your lover refuses to do what you ask.

The most effective sexual affirmations are highly specific. General affirmations like 'I am the perfect lover' or 'My lover finds me sexually irresistible' are fine for boosting sexual confidence, but they may not be specific enough to modify your behaviour. 'I love performing mind-blowing oral sex' or 'My body drives men wild' reflect a more success-ful strategy. Your inner mind more readily accepts programmes which state exactly what it needs to do to improve your sexual performance or pleasure. Formulate your affirmations with pinpoint precision, with a realistic understanding of your current sexual behaviour.

'I respond to sexual pleasure by creating orgasmic release' doesn't specify what type of orgasm-producing pleasure is needed (or desired). 'I have a tremendous orgasm whenever I let my lover penetrate my vagina' leaves little doubt as to what should occur. (Your sexual affirmation needn't sound like a quotation from a medical text. Use whatever words are familiar, comfortable and powerful.)

As long as it's specific, the sexual affirmation you choose is limited only by your imagination. You can improve your technique ('I know exactly how to move my hips to make my lover come'), focus your excitement ('My lover's ____ drives me wild with excitement'), try a new position ('I love making love from behind'), experiment with erot-ica ('I am turned on by reading other people's sexual experiences') or vary your sexual frequency ('I am hot and excited three times a week'). Once again, check your goal against your partner's needs. If your part-ner does not share your spirit of adventure, if he or she ridicules your changed sexual pattern, this 'negative reinforcement' could easily pre-vent any new programme from taking hold in your inner mind. However, if your partner welcomes a change of sexual programme, if he or she shares the benefits of your increased sexual satisfaction, you couldn't ask for more powerful positive reinforcement.

No matter how disappointing or dramatic the results, stay with one affirmation for a minimum of seven self-hypnosis sessions. Keep a record of how well your subconscious reprogramming is working, so that your inner mind is encouraged by your success. If your goal is highly subjective (e.g., 'I love making love to my lover the way she loves it'), rate your satisfaction on a scale of one to ten, and note if the rating improves over time. With this particular challenge, motivating yourself to test the success of your self-hypnosis should not be a prob-lem. As for the next step – creative visualisation – well, that's about as much fun as you can have with your clothes on . . .

Four Types of Affirmations

- **Emotional.** 'I love selling cars' or 'I feel calm, relaxed and happy when I'm with my boss'.

- **Inspirational.** 'My legs are so comfortable I can walk all the way to the shops' or 'I love flying to beautiful exotic places'.

- **Practical.** 'I find it perfectly easy to remember historical dates' or 'My breasts are growing larger'.

- **Directional.** 'I concentrate only on my pleasure when making love' or 'I focus my thoughts on all the good things in life'.

The Five Rules of Creating a Successful Affirmation

- **Only one at a time.**

- **Make it entirely positive.** Ineffective: 'I don't eat huge amounts of chocolate after work'. Effective: 'I enjoy eating fresh, healthy food after work'.

- **Keep it short.** Ineffective: 'I find it extremely easy to put my head down every night and drift off into a deep, relaxing sleep and always wake up refreshed and relaxed, ready to start my day'. Effective: 'I fall asleep easily and sleep peacefully'.

- **Make it specific and achievable.** Ineffective: 'I feel no pain'. Effective: 'My knees feel warm, comfortable and relaxed'.

- **Make it active.** Ineffective: 'I don't think about my problems'. Effective: 'I always think about all the wonderful things in my life'.

16

Success: Enjoy it Now to Create it Later

What can be conceived can be created. It's not simply a catchy saying designed to raise your expectations. It's literally true. Have you ever heard someone consider something new and say, 'Oh no, I can't see myself doing that. Me surfing? Can you just picture *me* in a bikini, standing on one of those boards? The very idea!' This all-too-common response is a failure of the imagination, and all new endeavours start with your imagination. If you can't imagine yourself doing something, you're finished before you start. Your mind will not address the technical considerations, or weigh the possible benefits against the potential disadvantages. At the end of the day, you won't even try. On the other hand, if you *can* imagine yourself doing something you've never done before, you're in with a chance. As Henry Ford said, 'If you think you can or you think you can't, you're right.'

During the Fifties, the American director of a top-secret rocket research programme put Henry Ford's maxim to the test. The director's team were trying to create a new type of engine. The project was going nowhere fast. Many of the engineers were convinced they were attempting the impossible. One day, the director showed the scientists a spy film of a secret Russian rocket engine. The Russians had solved the problem! Unfortunately, no-one knew how. Even so, the American scientists were re-energised. Within months, they'd cracked it. They had come up with their own solution. The project head then revealed that the Russian film was faked. Like Henry Ford, he knew his team could do the impossible as long as they didn't *think* it was impossible. If they could imagine a solution they would find it. And so they did.

Everything achieved by humanity started in someone's imagination: the electricity flowing through your home, the heat that keeps you warm, the cars outside your door, this book, your clothes, the carpet, the wallpaper – everything. If you have something you want to create, whether it's a set of shelves or a non-smoking lifestyle, you need to imagine it first. It seems simple enough: the first step to creating anything is deciding what 'it' is. Yet Western society tends to downplay the importance of our imagination. Want to get something done? Want to change your life? *Facts* are what's important. After all, what good is an idea if you don't have the facts, the scientific plan to make it reality? What are you going to do, *dream* something into existence? Well, yes, actually. That's what we're *already* doing, all day, every day.

Let's say you want to catch a train. The traditional way to approach the goal is to analyse the task factually. **Fact:** the train leaves the station at three p.m. **Fact:** it's two p.m. **Fact:** it takes half an hour to get to the station. **Fact:** if I leave now, I'll catch the train. Where's the imagination in that? First, you imagine the train. Then you imagine that you can catch the train. Then you imagine the route to the station. Then you imagine what will happen if you leave straightaway. Your motivation also depends on both fact and imagination. You could say you're taking a train because of the fact that your grandmother asked you to visit. Or you could say that you're taking the train because you can imagine that your grandmother would like to see you. Normally, we imagine something first, *then* apply our rational mind to the challenge of making it happen.

Although you can consciously decide to imagine something, and you can consciously think about what you're imagining, the vast majority of imagination occurs on the subconscious level. Imagining a train is so basic and familiar that you're not even aware you're doing it when you're making travel plans. To use a computer analogy, your imagination is the operating software that allows you to work with a computer programme. You don't think about all the computer instructions that let you tap a key to produce a letter on-screen. You think about what letters you want to type and what you want to say. In the same sense, people don't normally spend much time imagining their goal while working towards it. They get on with the business at hand. Yet the computer analogy isn't appropriate for personal achievement. To accomplish your goals, you need to get involved with the operating instructions of your inner mind. You need to imagine.

When I was first invited to speak on the radio, I decided I didn't want to deal with callers' problems on a purely rational level. I contacted the radio authority and asked them if I could hypnotise callers over the air. The authority said their regulations forbid either advertising or broadcasting hypnosis. In that case, could I ask callers to close their eyes and imagine something pleasant and relaxing? Could I inspire them with a vision of change? The authority gave me permission to use this technique. First, I talked to each caller about their problems to establish clear and positive goals. Then I told them to close their eyes and imagine a beautiful scene. Then I asked them to enjoy their future success: losing weight, sleeping peacefully, etc. Using this technique, I was able to cure two cases of insomnia, retrieve an important lost memory and inspire dozens of smokers and over-eaters towards change.

In some ways, imagination *is* hypnosis. When you imagine something, you establish a powerful link between your conscious and sub-conscious mind. My radio callers didn't need a twenty-minute hypnotic induction to access their inner mind. All they had to do was close their eyes and use their imagination. Try it. Imagine yourself thinner. With a little luck (or practice), your subconscious mind will immediately create a vision of a slimmer you. If you're looking for weight loss, let your conscious mind enjoy the image. Add an affirma-tion – send a conscious message back to your inner mind to help turn the vision into reality – and you're on your way. You've created a link between desire and change, imagination and creation. This process is often called 'creative visualisation'. Without hypnosis, it can be extremely effective. With hypnosis, creative visualisation is faster, stronger and more powerful.

With creative visualisation, you convince your inner mind that change is desirable, achievable and inevitable. You could spend a lot of time in self-hypnosis rationally explaining to your inner mind why, how and when it should change subconscious patterns. You could arrange an army of indisputable facts that would make the march from here (current behaviour) to there (new behaviour) seem fun, easy and worthwhile. Don't waste your time. When it comes to subcon-scious motivation, a picture is worth ten thousand words. The quick-est way to convince your inner mind to let go of an old pattern or try something new is to show your inner mind what life will be like once the change is made. Give it a vision of a happier, more satisfied and excited you. Since the inner mind always says 'yes', an inspiring vision of a better life is the ultimate 'carrot' for change. It puts all that subconscious 'yes' energy to work for change.

Want to be calm, confident and relaxed when asking for a rise in pay? Put yourself into self-hypnosis and imagine the scene. Imagine yourself calm, confident and relaxed. Want to walk without any pain in your knees? Picture yourself walking comfortably. For instant inner motivation, make your imaginary scene one where your new behav-iour is earning you *enormous* rewards: respect, a pay rise, undying love, whatever. Visualise yourself calmly discussing your work with your boss, who is so impressed he gives you a rise on the spot.

Visualise yourself walking easily down the high street, going to buy some beautiful new clothes. If you really enjoy living your new, improved life in trance, your inner mind will have the incentive it needs to create the success in reality.

Creative visualisation and hypnosis combine perfectly because a hypnotised inner mind can't make fine distinctions between past, present and future. Equally, trance blurs the concepts of 'imaginary' and 'real'. Put yourself into a deep trance and imagine you're on a plane; relaxed, calm and happy. When is it happening? Now, later or at no fixed time? Are you *really* on a plane or sitting in a chair imagining you're on a plane? The inner mind isn't bothered analysing creative visualisations for the 'truth'. It doesn't matter. As long as the vision is enjoyable, the inner mind will go along for the ride. By telling your subconscious mind what to do (the affirmation) then showing it the benefits of doing what you ask (visualisation), you create a deeply held belief. Once your inner mind believes something is possible, it's only a matter of time before you achieve it.

The power of a deeply held belief is almost beyond measure. Early Christians were known for the amazing strength of their convictions. They would not renounce their faith even under the most hideous torture. Baptism may have been the reason. Baptism was once a secret ceremony with only the priest and the congregant present. Both participants would take off their clothes, cross the river Jordan and visit Heaven. It's not clear if the priest used a form of hypnosis, but the baptised Christian would then believe that he or she had literally seen Heaven. This vision of paradise created a deeply held belief: Christian faith leads to a real Heaven ruled by a living God. Armed with this faith, the Christians could overcome persecution to spread their message. Even the threat of death in the Roman Colosseum couldn't shake the power of their baptismal vision or the belief it sustained.

On a less spiritual level, creative visualisation is mental rehearsal. Like the old joke says, how do you get to the Albert Hall? Practice! How do you change subconscious patterns? Practice! Millions of people faithfully practise tennis and golf. Yet when they face an event where their subconscious mind has a history of negative behaviour – a business presentation, aeroplane flight or romantic date – they try to successfully 'wing it'. How can you expect to perform well at something challenging when you haven't prepared? I treated an actress for opening-night nerves. While she had rehearsed her part to perfection, she had never rehearsed the opening night itself. By hypnotising her and guiding her through a triumphant (if imaginary) first night, I helped her feel calm and relaxed at the 'real' performance. Like any good rehearsal, creative visualisation prepares you for success.

Are you trying to give up cigarettes once and for all? Visualise yourself breathing fresh, clean air in a situation where you normally light up. Do you have a fear of open spaces that imprisons you in your own home? Visualise yourself walking out of your front door into the wide world, living a normal life. Chocolate bars keeping you from losing weight? Visualise yourself in your local newsagent, ignoring those rows of brightly coloured high-calorie confections. Exam nerves standing between you and academic success? Visualise yourself cool as cucumber during your exams. Nervous on dates? Visualise yourself as irresistibly seductive. Business presentations bring you out in a cold sweat? Visualise yourself in a meeting being calm, masterful and persuasive. Creative visualisation is the single best way to convince your inner mind that it *can* do what you want it to do. What can be conceived can be created.

Instructions

Creative visualisation is the last step in your self-hypnosis programme. If you like to fantasise, this is the treat for all the relaxation discipline you've had to master. If you don't like to fantasise or have fallen out of practice since childhood, this is your opportunity to relearn the limitless pleasures of your own imagination. First, a quick review:

Step 1: Relax Your Mind and Body
(approximately 5 minutes)

Tug your ear lobe, say 'sleep' and close your eyes. Adjust your breathing and/or practise progressive relaxation. Step 1 removes you from the 'real world', relieves physical and mental stress and focuses both conscious and subconscious mind.

Step 2: Deepen the Trance
(approximately 2 minutes)

Imagine going down stairs. Step 2 takes you away from all your cares, worries and doubts. It deepens the trance by instructing your inner mind gradually to increase your natural relaxation.

Step 3: Imagine Your Special Place
(approximately 5 minutes)

Create a pleasurable environment for the inner mind to receive new instructions. Step 3 gives you all the benefits of a mental holiday.

Step 4: Repeat Your Affirmation Five Times
(approximately 1 minute)

Tell your inner mind exactly what you want it to do. Step 4 re-programmes your inner mind for success.

Step 5: Creative Visualisation
(approximately 6 minutes)

Imagine your success now to achieve it later. Step 5 reinforces the new subconscious programme and motivates the inner mind to change.

Creative visualisation begins with the idea that your affirmation is true. You *are* calm, confident and relaxed. You *have* the perfect breasts. You *love* spiders. The cancer *is* gone. Once your inner mind accepts this starting point, leave your special place for a 'real' place where you can practise living your affirmation. There are two basic types of scenes or locations to choose from: *practical* and *inspirational*.

Practical scenes offer the most direct form of subconscious reprogramming. You recall a real situation where your subconscious mind got it wrong, then you imagine yourself in the same situation getting it totally right. For example, if your affirmation is 'I eat the perfect amount of food at dinner parties', you visualise yourself at a dinner party eating the perfect amount of food. If your affirmation is 'My skin is smooth as silk in the mornings', you visualise yourself looking at a clear complexion in the bathroom mirror some sunny morning. Practical scenes are both a full dress rehearsal and a full set of non-verbal instructions for your inner mind. Practical creative visualisation re-trains the inner mind by showing it exactly what to do.

Inspirational scenes are less like a 'how-to' guide and more like a glitzy bestseller. You visualise yourself successful in a fantasy setting. In the weight-loss example above, a woman could visualise herself slim and sexy at the world's most glittering dinner party: exotic location, sparkling crystal, fine china, fresh flowers, celebrities, royalty, etc. Inspirational scenes needn't take place where the affirmation suggests; they can be entirely based on future and/or imaginary rewards. A businessman who uses 'I easily convince customers to buy our products' can imagine buying a new Ferrari with his earnings. A person using 'I pass all my law exams with top-class results' can imagine winning an important case. Subconscious change can sometimes be a long and difficult struggle; inspirational scenes are a constant reminder to your inner mind of why you should stay with it.

Whether you choose a practical or inspirational visualisation, start by imagining the details. If you're at a dinner party, check out the table. What kind of silver, flowers and china can you see? What are you wearing? Who's with you? Can you smell their cologne or perfume? If you're buying a Ferrari, take a good look at the salesperson. How are they dressed? What's the leather steering wheel feel like? If you're in court, what case are you working on? Who's there? What kind of paper are you using for your notes? Try to use as many imaginary senses as possible. By focusing on the small details of your scene, you convince your inner mind of the reality of the scene.

Then it's time to roll the cameras. You're the lead in your very own success story! Your creative visualisation is an imaginary slice of your life story with a beginning, middle and end. Run through your success in 'real time', from start to finish. Just as there is no room for doubt in your affirmation, there is no room for failure in your creative visualisation. *Visualise everything that happens as a total success.* Go ahead, go 'over the top'. Anything is possible. Dare to imagine the unimaginable. If you're not used to visualising yourself, it may be a little difficult at first. Many people wonder if they should visualise themselves from the outside (second person) or imagine the scene 'from the inside' (first person). It doesn't matter. You can even switch back and forth between first and second person – as long as you're the star!

Creative visualisation is great therapy, but it should also be great fun. If you awake from your visualisation with a smile on your face, you're definitely on the right track. With the creative-visualisation exercise, your entire self-hypnosis session should take about twenty minutes. Use the wake-up script in Chapter Fourteen and you're finished! Of course, in some ways, you've just started. You can apply the self-hypnosis technique to just about any challenge that surfaces in your life. Once you master the technique, you can spend the rest of your life refining, improving and experimenting with the process. Never forget that it's more important to do it, than to do it right.

17

Deeper and Deeper . . .

You now have the basics. You can now put yourself into a trance, re-programme your inner mind, imagine your success and wake yourself up. That's about all you need to change your life. By this point, you should be practising daily self-hypnosis. Provided you've set a short-term, measurable goal *and* you've passed the two-week mark, you should be seeing changes in thought, behaviour or physical reactions. If you are experiencing the benefits of subconscious modification, this chapter will help you extend your hypnotic depth and range. If you're not seeing results, experiment with the variables described in previous chapters: hypnotic voice, pace, creative suggestion, affirmation and visualisation. There is enormous scope for improvement within your existing abilities. Then try some of the ideas described here.

Advanced Deepening Technique

The staircase and its cousins (lifts, escalators, etc.) are gradual deepening techniques. They depend on the *law of increasing effect*: your mind's ability to amplify a small shift in consciousness to make it more and more powerful. While gradually soothing yourself into deeper and deeper relaxation is very effective, you can also jolt your inner mind into a deeper trance. The short form is amazingly simple. You put yourself in trance, then say: 'On the count of three, I will sink deeper. One. Two. Three.' Make sure you pause a good ten seconds to feel the effect. Try repeating the technique several times in a row. Or centre your mind on any image which suggests a sudden 'dive' into a deeper trance, such as a leap off a towering cliff or a dive into a clear pool. Tell your inner mind what's going to happen, count to three and go for it.

One of the best of the instant deepening methods is the 'The Starseeker' technique. Tug your ear lobe, say 'sleep' and close your eyes. Modify your breathing and practise a bit of progressive relaxation. When you're ready, use the following script as a guide; you can also record the script on to a tape and play it back in trance. Once again, change the script from 'you' to 'I' if you prefer addressing your subconscious in the first person. Above all, take your time!

1. Walk through a field

Imagine you're walking through a beautiful field on a warm summer's night. There's nowhere to go and nothing to do. You're alone and safe, just walking through the field. All the world is at rest. The air smells sweet and perfumed. You're perfectly comfortable. You can hear the grass rustle softly in the warm night air. Imagine there's a full moon, bathing everything around you in soft, pale, moonlight.

2. Some place to relax

You're so warm and safe and comfortable. It's such a beautiful night. You want to find some place to just sit down and relax. Look around, and find some place to just sit down and relax. Some place really comfortable. Where you can just stretch out and rest. Where you can enjoy the warm summer's night. Find some place really comfortable, stretch out, and relax.

3. Look up

Now look up. Look up, at the billions of stars, stretched out, across the infinite blackness of space. Stars like a billion diamonds, spread out, across an endless piece of velvet. *Feel* the same sense of wonder that you felt as a child. The same sense of wonder you felt when you were a child, looking up into a beautiful night sky. Wonder at being part of something so *enormous*. And, at the same time, being something small and precious. Like a candle in a dark room.

4. Messages of peace

Notice that the stars all seem to be beaming you messages. Messages of peace. Messages of relaxation. Messages of _____ (your challenge: weight loss, stopping smoking, etc.). All the stars are telling you to relax. Everything is going to be just fine. Everything is going to be exactly as it should be. Stars telling you that you can *really* relax. That all your problems are not really all that important. You can really relax and let go.

5. One star

Notice that one star is a little bit brighter than all the rest. Notice that this star's messages are more powerful, more personal, than all the rest. And notice that this star is growing in the night sky. The larger this star becomes, the more powerful and personal its messages become. Growing stronger and stronger.

6.   Ready to dive in

This star will grow larger and larger, until it is so large that you'll just have to dive in. When you dive in, you'll let go of everything. I'm going to count to five. By the number five, the star will be so large that you will just dive in and let go. Let go of everything.

7.   Countdown

(*NB: use a forceful hypnotic voice and increase the tempo as you go along*)

ONE: The star is about half as big as the full moon. It has a brighter whiter light than the pale moonlight.

TWO: The star is as large as the full moon. Which means it is very, very large in the night sky. So large you feel yourself being sucked towards it.

THREE: It's bigger than the full moon now. It's bigger than any-thing you've ever seen in the night sky. It's changing the way every-thing looks around you. Everything is blanketed in a very bright, white light.

FOUR: It's absolutely enormous now. You feel yourself being sucked straight off the planet surface, straight into the heart of this intensely bright white light. Getting ready to jump in and let go. And . . .

FIVE: Jump in and *let go! Let go of everything. Let go of your past and your future. Let go of your physical body. Let go of all your cares and worries and doubts. Let go as you dive into the bright white light. It's inside you, it's outside you. You're breathing it in, and you're breathing it out. You're like a fish in an ocean of perfect relaxation. It may be an idea, an image, a thought, a word – it doesn't matter. However you feel this relaxation, jump in and let go. Let go! Let go of everything! As you let go, feel yourself sinking deeper and deeper, deeper and deeper, deeper and deeper into perfect relaxation.*

(From this point on, gradually slow down your pace and soften your tone.)

Really letting go now. Really feeling relaxed. Relaxed and calm. Nice and relaxed and calm. More and more relaxed. Letting go and relaxing deeper. Letting go. Letting go. Letting go of everything. Just letting go and drifting. Drifting and floating. Floating and drifting. Down. Deeper and deeper and deeper down. Down. Down. Down. You are now perfectly relaxed. The white light is gradually replaced with the yellow light of our star. The sun. The sun shining in your special place. You are now in your special place. Nice and relaxed and calm in your special place.

Advanced Tests

There are scientific devices which can monitor the physiological changes which routinely occur in a trance state. You can use these devices to measure falling heartrate, changing brain waves and changing body temperature. Yet it's impossible to establish a reliable connection between any physical response and trance depth. As scientists feel lost without *some* kind of objective yardstick, they decided that the best way to measure trance depth is by its effects. If you can be made to forget your name, you must be in a pretty deep trance. If you can't, you aren't. It's like measuring wind speed by tossing a piece of paper in the air. If it drops straight to the ground, it's not windy. If it flies off, it is.

You *can* get a rough idea of how deep a trance you're working with by seeing what you can do with it. Whenever I hypnotise someone, I use hypnotic tests to tell me if the client's subconscious mind is following my instructions. Depending on their response, I know whether to deepen the trance, gently suggest some new ideas or forcefully command a subconscious change. Even better, successful tests *create* trance depth. They prove to a subject that they are in a hypnotic state. A convinced client usually relaxes and sinks down into an even deeper trance. A successful hypnotic test is also a miniature version of hypnotherapy: setting and achieving a goal using the subconscious mind. It shows the client the exact process which will change their life.

Whatever does or does not happen with the following tests, don't get fixated on the results. Your new life doesn't depend on them. It depends on hypnotic repetition and belief.

Advanced Finger Levitation Test

This test was originally introduced in Chapter Twelve as a way to measure hypnotic response *before* trance. As the trance state makes your inner mind more suggestible, the Finger-Raise Test should be even more effective in trance. First, tug your ear lobe, say 'sleep' and close your eyes. Adjust your breathing, deepen the trance using one of the methods you've learned, then use this script (or its rough equivalent) to create the advanced levitation effect. This time you're trying to levitate the entire arm. As always, feel free to switch the wording from 'my' to 'your', depending on your preference.

Advanced Finger Levitation Script

1. First finger

I am now concentrating on my index finger on my _____ (right/left) hand. And as I concentrate on my index finger, the finger is getting lighter and lighter. The lighter my finger gets, the deeper I sink into trance. The deeper I sink into trance, the lighter my finger gets.

My finger is getting lighter and lighter. Light like a bird rising up on a warm gust of wind. Light like I'm pumping helium gas into my finger with each breath out. Light like there's a balloon tied to the end of the finger, gently tugging it up. A balloon tied to my finger gently tugging it up. Up. Higher and higher. Lighter and lighter. Lighter and lighter. Higher and lighter. Sinking deeper and deeper as my finger rises higher and higher, etc.

[Keep repeating these ideas – or your own – until the finger starts to rise. Stay with it! Let your finger rise right up. Once the finger is at its height, move on to the next part of the script.]

2. All the fingers

This feeling of lightness is now spreading to the other fingers in my hand. All the fingers in my _____ (right/left) hand are getting lighter. All the fingers are starting to rise up. Getting lighter and lighter. Rising straight up, as I sink deeper and deeper, feeling more and more relaxed. All the other fingers also have helium balloons tied to them, gently pulling them up. Up higher. Lighter and higher, etc.

[Continue after all the fingers being to rise . . .]

3. Entire hand

Now my entire hand, right up to my wrist, is starting to rise up. The feeling of lightness spreading right into the entire hand. The hand is wanting to rise up now. Getting lighter and lighter, as I sink deeper and deeper into trance. The deeper I go, the lighter it becomes. The lighter it becomes, the deeper I go. Lighter and deeper. Deeper and lighter. Rising right up off the _____ (chair/sofa/lap).

[Continue after the hand lifts up . . .]

4. Arm

And now my arm. The feeling of lightness spreading right up my arm
to my elbow. My whole arm's lifting off now. Lifting off like a rocket
lifting off into space. My whole arm weightless, rising up. Rising right
up. I'm sinking deeper and deeper into trance. Way down, as my arm
goes way up. Deeper and higher. Lighter and lighter.

[Continue after the arm lifts up . . .]

5. Towards the face

My hand is now attracted towards my face. My fingers are moving
towards my face. Like a magnet and a piece of metal, my hands are
irresistibly drawn towards my face. Getting closer and closer. When
my fingers touch my face, I'll drop my hand and sink into my deepest
trance. Hand moving closer. Ready to drop into a deep trance. Closer
and closer. Closer and closer, etc.

[When your fingers touch your face, let your hand drop. Leave your
hand where it falls for a minute or so. Then, if you like, move your
hand and arm back into a more comfortable position. The test finishes
here. Continue your self-hypnosis with your special place, affirmation,
creative visualisation and wake up.]

Rating the Advanced Finger/Arm Levitation

Nothing happens	1
Just one finger rises up	2
All fingers rise up, but that's all	3
Your hand rises up as well, but that's all	4
Your arm rises up with difficulty, but that's all	5
Your arm rises up easily, but that's all	6
Your hand touches your face after *more* than five minutes	7
Your hand touches your face in *less* than five minutes	8
Your hand touches your face within three minutes	9
Your hand touches your face within two minutes	10

If you score between one and five, you are in a light trance. Keep practising! If you score between six and eight, you are in a medium trance.
If you score a nine or ten, you are in a deep trance.

Eyelid Catalepsy Test

One of the most impressive aspects of hypnosis is its ability to create
total muscular rigidity, called 'catalepsy'. Some stage hypnotists will

instruct the subject's subconscious to make their entire body 'as rigid as a bar of steel'. The hypnotist then places the subject's head on one chair and their feet on another, with nothing in between. The subject's body is so rigid that they lay across the two chairs like a plank of wood. With this test, you're focusing the inner mind on your eyelids to create catalepsy. The goal is to make them 'seal shut'.

Tug your ear lobe, say the word 'sleep' and close your eyes. Put yourself into a deep trance, then use the following script as your guideline.

Eyelid Catalepsy Script

1.   Sleep on the beach

I'm lying on a beautiful, warm beach.* I'm stretched out in the warm sun. Lying on a beautiful sandy white beach. There's no place to go and nothing to do. I'm just relaxing. I'm so relaxed that I'm closing my eyes. I'm drifting off into a deep sleep. A deep, relaxing sleep.

2.   Eyes warm and soothed and relaxed

And as I sleep peacefully, I can feel the warm sun on my eyes. The warm sun is soothing and warming and relaxing my eyes. My eyes are soothed and warm and relaxed.

3.   Eye muscles relaxed

The warm sun is bathing and soothing and relaxing all the muscles that control my eyes, and my eyelids. All the muscles that control my eyes and my eyelids are bathed and soothed and warm and relaxed.

4.   Eyes loose and limp and relaxed

The warm sun is bathing and soothing and relaxing all the muscles that control my eyes and my eyelids. So now my eyes are loose and limp and relaxed. My eyes are warmed, bathed, soothed, loose, limp and relaxed.

[Increase your pace and switch to a more forceful hypnotic voice.]

5.   Sealed shut

My eyes are now so warm and bathed and soothed and loose and limp and relaxed that they are sealed shut. My eyes are now sealed shut. Sealed shut. Glued shut. My eyes are sealed shut like they've been taped shut and glued shut. My eyes are now *sealed shut*. They are

* If you don't like beaches, choose some other place that's nice and warm and sunny. If you don't like the sun, modify this script to take out references to direct sunlight.

warmed and bathed and soothed and loose and limp and relaxed *and completely sealed shut.*

6. I can *try* to open them but . . .

I can try to open my eyes, but I won't be able to. Because my eyes are completely sealed shut. I will count to three and try and open my eyes, but I won't be able to. Because they are sealed shut.

7. Test

One. Two. Three! I can't open my eyes because they are completely sealed shut. The harder I try, the more they're sealed shut.

8. Stop trying

I will now stop trying and relax into a deeper state of perfect relaxation. My eyes are completely back to normal, but I'll keep them shut until I wake up from trance.

Rating the Eyelid Catalepsy Test

- **Pass.** Eyelids seal shut, can't open them. Medium to deep trance.
- **Try again.** Eyes open. Light trance.

The Associative Post-Hypnotic Suggestion

The Associative Post-Hypnotic Suggestion (APHS) is the 'mother of all hypnotic tests'. To create an APHS, put yourself into trance. Then you give your subconscious a highly specific command or 'suggestion'. Something along the lines of, 'I will say the word "banana" any time the phone rings' or 'I will feel an irresistible urge to change my shoes at exactly ten p.m.'. You're commanding your inner mind to associate a specific trigger (telephone, ten p.m.) with a specific response ('banana', shoes). Then you wake yourself up and (post-hypnotically) expose yourself to the trigger. Providing it works, your inner mind will automatically carry out the new subconscious programme. You say the word 'banana' whenever the phone rings or change your shoes at ten p.m. *whether you want to or not.*

Once again, this is a fairly tricky concept. Don't make it too complicated. If you follow the command, the APHS worked. If you don't, it didn't.

This is usually the most convincing test for subjects. It proves to them that they were 'under'. Performing the test couldn't be easier. Just tug your ear lobe, say the word 'sleep' and close your eyes. Deepen the trance, go to your special place and relax. Before your affirmation, give your subconscious mind a very specific command. The APHS can be designed to trigger physical sensation: 'Whenever I look at my doorknob, my head will itch'. It can trigger time distortion: 'Tonight's television news will seem to take forever'. It can trigger future behaviour: 'I will wake up at exactly eight a.m. tomorrow morning'. It can trigger emotional states: 'I will be really angry for fifteen minutes after my tea'. It can trigger a thought: 'Whenever someone says "Niagara Falls", I will think of my wife.'

The type of APHS you use is limited only by the need to create a response you can check and your imagination. *Don't make yourself do anything stupid, dangerous or embarrassing.* The inner mind will reject this type of command. The worst thing that could happen is that it *doesn't* reject the negative APHS. Self-hypnosis is based on trust between your conscious and subconscious minds. If you humiliate your inner mind, it will quickly view self-hypnosis as an elaborate trick and reject *all* suggestions.

After you've given your subconscious an APHS, finish your self-hypnosis session as normal. If you really want to implant the APHS deeply, skip the affirmation and visualise yourself carrying out the APHS. Then wake yourself up.

Rating the Associative Post-Hypnotic Suggestion

If the Associative Post-Hypnotic Suggestion works, if you carry out the new command, you were in a deep trance. If the APHS doesn't work, you need a deeper trance and more practice. Note that some subconscious minds are a bit slower than others. If you used the APHS 'Whenever I pick up my pen, my nose will itch', you may not notice an immediate effect. However, perhaps five to ten minutes later, you may find yourself scratching your nose. Give your inner mind time to respond.

WARNING!
YOU MUST REMOVE AN UNWANTED APHS

An Associative Post-Hypnotic Suggestion creates a new subconscious programme. Providing your inner mind accepts the programme, *it will stay accepted.* An APHS like, 'Whenever I pick up my pen, my nose will itch' means exactly that. Wherever you are, whatever you're doing, for the rest of your life, your nose will itch when you pick up your pen. (Your inner mind is very literal as well, so it's *your* pen, not *a* pen.) To remove the APHS, put yourself back in trance and reprogramme your inner mind: 'Whenever I pick up my pen, my nose will remain comfortable.'

The Associative Post-Hypnotic Suggestion (APHS) as Therapy

The Associative Post-Hypnotic Suggestion could well be the most useful hypnotherapy technique you can learn. For therapeutic APHS, do your normal self-hypnosis session, then insert the command before your wake-up script. *Always use the preamble: 'From this moment on . . '* Here are two commands that you should implant in your inner mind as soon as possible:

• **'From this moment on, any time I tug my ear lobe and say the word "sleep" I will sink into a deep, relaxing trance.'**
This command provides a quick and easy way back into trance. Begin every self-hypnosis suggestion with the ear-lobe tug to reinforce the suggestion.

• **'From this moment on, whenever I touch my thumb and index finger together, stare at an object and take two slow breaths, I will feel a perfect wave of relaxation through my mind and body.'**

This command gives you a mental calming technique to use whenever you need. Use the Finger Touch Technique at least twice a day to reinforce the suggestion. Keep 'the wave' standing by.

Like a good affirmation, a well-designed APHS reprogrammes your brain for success. However, while an affirmation roots out and replaces a bad subconscious programme, an APHS simply inserts a new one. It's a subtle but important difference. If you're afraid of flying, an affirmation like 'I love flying to exotic places' followed by an exciting creative visualisation will diminish or eliminate your phobia. An APHS like 'From this moment on, whenever I sit on an aeroplane seat, I feel relaxed and calm' is less likely to be powerful enough to over-ride or replace the faulty programme. Instead, use the APHS 'quick fix' to help you directly control/avoid the negative subconscious response: 'From this moment on, whenever I sit on an aeroplane seat, my breathing slows down' or 'From this moment on, whenever I sit on an aeroplane seat, I fall into a deep, restful sleep'.

When framing your goal-specific APHS, try to stay within the boundaries of what's possible while challenging your subconscious mind to deliver. Give yourself something easy enough so that you're likely to follow the command, but not so easy that the result will be boring. Also, experiment with linking your APHS to a specific hypnotic phenomena: 'From this moment on, whenever I see a packet of cigarettes, I think of watching my children grow up' or 'From this moment on, whenever I taste something sweet, I immediately feel full' or 'From this moment on, whenever I'm in an important meeting, time slows down so that I have all the time I need'. Decide what change will help you towards your goal, then command your inner mind to make the change.

It's that easy to change your life.

18

Failure is Impossible!

Practising self-hypnosis with these techniques is like cooking from a recipe: the instructions may be the same for everyone, but the results will vary. I've listed all the ingredients you need to change your subconscious programming. I've described a recipe for combining these elements for maximum effect in minimum time. But I can't guarantee that self-hypnosis will be as easy as pie. There are simply too many unknown factors: the extent of the problem, how badly you want or need to change, your hypnotisability and more. As a professional hypnotherapist, I've learned that there is no one thing called 'a smoker' or 'someone with a drugs problem' and that words like 'depression' or 'anxiety' are meaningless except as a cry for help. Everyone experiences their problem in their own unique way. Everyone solves their problem in their own unique way. I can show you how it's done, but I can't do it for you. *You* are the chef.

Although your success is down to you, the nice thing about working to a recipe is that someone's done it before. Using altered states of mind to overcome personal challenges is as old as mankind itself. Long before the healing arts became a science, people depended on the power of their inner mind to see them through the worst that nature (human and Mother) could throw at them. The trance state has always been the place where mind and spirit join together to fight sickness and disease. In many parts of the world, the power of the inner mind is still the best weapon in the fight for health and happiness. Sometimes, it's all people can afford. Sometimes, it's all they need. When you practise your self-hypnosis, rest assured that you are boldly going where millions have gone before. Whether tapping into your inner mind works quickly for you remains to be seen. At least you're not exploring virgin territory. At least you're not alone.

If you take a wrong turn in your journey into your inner mind or find yourself stuck in a quiet little cul-de-sac, don't panic or despair. While your experience of self-hypnosis is unique, your difficulties probably aren't. When I run group sessions, participants often face the same problems at the same time. When one client keeps falling asleep on the way to their special place, a couple of others are also struggling to stay awake. When one person finds their visualisation fuzzy and uninspirational, someone else is also having trouble imagining their success. If you're using this book by yourself, reprogramming your subconscious mind is enough of a challenge without wondering if you're somehow hypnotically defective. You aren't. Whatever difficulties you may encounter, they're probably not unusual or insurmountable. As long as you keep trying, you *will* find a way forward.

The following questions come from people who practised self-hypnosis and found themselves wandering off the path to change. The answers will help put you back on track. Obviously, you may encounter an obstacle (or two) that has nothing to do with any of the challenges described here. If so, apply the two rules of hypnotic problem-solving:

• **Relax.** There may not be a problem. Change takes time and you may not have given yourself enough. Perseverance and patience may be all you need.

• **Try something different.** If a key doesn't turn in a lock, try another key. As the American inventor Thomas Edison said, nothing is more important to success than failure. Each solution that doesn't work brings you one solution closer to one that does.

I keep falling asleep. What should I do?

The trance state is not sleep. In fact, your mind should be *more* active in trance than when you're doing something tiring like housework or last-minute shopping. However, the feeling of pure relaxation you create in self-hypnosis is certainly a lot closer to sleep than ironing shirts or walking down a crowded street. If you're tired, your subconscious mind may use the relaxation created in self-hypnosis as a bridge to the sleep state. It may gradually ignore your conscious commands until it gently drifts off into the world of dreams. For those suffering from insomnia, this is no bad thing. For people trying to reprogramme their inner mind to overcome another challenge, it is. You need to be fully awake to train your subconscious mind to respond to your command.

If you keep falling asleep in self-hypnosis, there are a few common sense steps you can take to keep yourself awake. First, get more sleep. Generally speaking, your subconscious knows what's good for you. When it seizes on self-hypnosis as a chance for forty winks, it's usually because your mind and body *need* the extra sleep. If the amount of hours you sleep varies over the week, try to establish a regular sleeping pattern. If you are in a regular pattern, try adding sleep in half-hour increments. Second, check your stress levels. The sleep response in trance could also be a signal that your mind and body are over-burdened. When you're suffering from long-term stress, the trance state becomes an opportunity for your subconscious to shut the whole system off for much-needed rest and recuperation. To avoid sleep in trance, you may need to work less and relax more. When was the last time you had a really relaxing vacation or a weekend break– not a non-stop or child-intensive adventure?

On the other hand, falling asleep in trance could just be a bad habit. Breaking the habit could be as easy as changing the time of your self-hypnosis. Most people practise self-hypnosis after work and before dinner, or the last thing at night. That can be a big mistake – you're too hungry or tired to concentrate. Try putting yourself in trance after your morning coffee, on the train to work or before lunch. Like swimming and public speaking, it's best not to practise self-hypnosis for an hour or so after a meal. The old subconscious 'eat-then-sleep' programme implanted when you were a baby is fiendishly hard to resist. Staying awake during self-hypnosis can also be as simple as adding a hypnotic command at the beginning of the session: 'The more relaxed I feel, the more awake and alert I become' or 'As I go down these stairs, I will feel more and more refreshed and wide awake'.

If you're still slipping off to sleep, make your self-hypnosis shorter and punchier. Experiment. Play around with the running order, perhaps starting with creative visualisation and working your way backwards to controlled breathing. Try hypnotising yourself out loud. Use rock 'n' roll rather than New Age music as a sonic background. If all else fails, do your self-hypnosis with your eyes open while staring at a candle or some other focal point. Distracting your inner mind away from sleep may take some practice or radical intervention, but it's well worth the effort. When it comes to changing your life, trance time is not nap time.

I can't seem to find the time for self-hypnosis. How do I motivate myself to stay with this?

The number of clients who swear they can't find twenty minutes a day for self-hypnosis is quite staggering. After all, these are the same clients who somehow found the time to contact the clinic, battle through London traffic and spend an hour in hypnotherapy. If a client honestly can't find twenty minutes to spare in an average day, they should be concerned about their stress levels. Humans are not machines; we *need* free time. Normally, what the clients are *really* saying is that they can't be bothered. If that's the case, so be it. As discussed in the chapter on motivation, if something inside is saying 'no thanks', maybe you should listen. If the whole self-hypnosis process seems like a lot of effort for minimum reward, then don't do it. There are many ways to cure a problem which don't involve taking twenty minutes a day to sit alone, relax and think. Put HypnoHealth somewhere safe. Come back to it when you're ready.

Some people really do want to practise self-hypnosis, but can't seem to get it together. For those struggling for self-discipline, it's important to spend more time getting excited about change and less time trying to create it. Skip all the initial stages of self-hypnosis and go straight to creative visualisation. Imagine your success in every detail. See how much better your life will be once you've conquered your challenge. Don't spend more than five minutes on this exercise, but do it as frequently and in as many situations as possible. Then gradually add the other stages, in whatever order you like. While self-hypnosis should ideally be practised the same way every day until you achieve your goal, if you are bored with this kind of repetition, experiment. Better to do it 'wrong' than not to do it. Your own style could well be more effective than the one recommended here.

The hypnotic buddy system is another way to motivate yourself. Find someone else who faces the same challenge. Buy them a copy of this book. Tell them you're thinking about giving self-hypnosis a try. Discuss the issues involved, then ask if they'd like to try it with you. The easiest way to 'buddy-up' is for both of you to practise at the same time every day. After your sessions, call each other on the phone and discuss how it went. Did your hand levitate? What affirmation are you using? Did you go deep that time? Are you losing weight? If you can arrange it, practise self-hypnosis side-by-side. The hypnotic energy of two people in trance relaxing towards the same goal at the same time is very powerful. Or you can read the scripts to each other. Although you're doing something serious, keep it fun and exciting. Changing your life should be a liberating experience.

Am I really *in a trance? How do I know?*

I've answered this question throughout the book with practical advice and hypnotic tests. Re-read the sections on trance depth and re-take the tests. Still, I know that many beginners find the 'am I? – aren't I?' question the single most worrying aspect of self-hypnosis. Once again, *you probably are in trance*. Once again, *it really doesn't matter*. Hypnosis is simply a relaxed state of mind and body characterised by suggestibility (your inner mind does what it's told to do). Providing you feel relaxed and providing you are achieving your well-defined, short-term goals, you're doing the business. Unless you're trying to become a professional hypnotic subject, the quality of your trance state is an entirely personal matter between you and your subconscious.

At the end of the day, asking if you're *really* in trance is like asking if you're *really* awake. Any answer is going to be so subjective as to be meaningless. The more important question is: Do you enjoy the feeling you get when you practise self-hypnosis? Do whatever it takes to make this trance-inducing technique an accustomed pleasure. Let your inner mind take care of the rest.

I can't 'see' myself in my visualisation. What do I do?

Your imagination is like a muscle: if you don't use it regularly it becomes weak and flabby. Although children spend more than half of their time in a trance-like state imagining all sorts of wild fantasies, adults aren't encouraged to keep their imagination strong and limber. Most jobs emphasise punctuality and conformity rather than creativity or imagination. Social interaction focuses on what you have and what you do, not what you can imagine. The popular culture of cinema and TV bloat us on a steady diet of pre-digested fantasies. Thankfully, the 'leave it to us we can imagine it for you' attitude of Western society is rapidly changing. More and more people make their living from the fruits of their imagination. Meanwhile, there are millions of people wandering around with little or no imaginative ability.

The creative visualisation exercise itself will help put your imagination back into shape. Your imagination will get better and better as the 'muscle' strengthens with use. If you really can't see anything in your mind's eye, go back to basics and work your way towards full visualisation. Start by spending a few minutes throughout your day imagining something static like a flower or pen. Take a good look at the object, then close your eyes and imagine it. After a few moments, open your eyes and check your internal image against the external actuality. Progress to something that moves, like a dog or a tree swaying in the breeze. Then imagine yourself. Start by standing in front of a mirror, creating and imagining various expressions. Move on to imagining yourself in certain situations. Try imagining yourself from the 'inside out' (seeing from your own eyes) and the 'outside in' (seeing yourself from the outside).

The video camera offers tremendous creative visualisation training.

First, have someone make several two-minute video segments of you doing something pleasant. Watch each segment on the tape one at a time, at least ten times each. Then close your eyes and replay the segment in your mind's eye. Keep at it until you can imagine each segment in any order you choose. Next, make your own series of two-minute videos of you walking (slowly) through somewhere beautiful and relaxing, like a favourite park or your back garden. Once again, watch each segment ten times, then close your eyes and imagine the scene. One advantage to video-style visualisation is that you can add special effects to your creative visualisation; you can freeze-frame a particularly inspiring image, zoom-in on something beautiful or picture your triumph in *Chariots of Fire*-like slow motion.

Creative visualisation is second nature to some, a lost skill to others. If you can't 'see' something by imagining it, imagine you can. With practice, you will.

I'm just not getting the results I want. What do I do now?

Many people seem to live by the motto that 'anything that's worth having is worth having now'. In a way that's true. Once you've fixed your mind on a goal, why wait? The sooner you do what you need to do to get what you want to get, the better. Self-hypnosis is a way to achieve health and happiness. There's not a moment to lose! The sooner you start your daily practice, the sooner you'll overcome your challenge. Unfortunately, that may not seem soon enough. I can't emphasise enough that self-hypnosis is a skill like any other; it requires a fair amount of patience and perseverance to master. Every day you practise self-hypnosis, you'll get a little better at using the trance state to achieve your goal. There's just no substitute for experience.

If you're not achieving the results you want, you've either got to keep the faith or change the goal. As you need *some* success to keep the faith, you might want to forget the main goal for a bit – at least until you prove to yourself the power of self-hypnosis. Use your self-hypnosis to change something trivial, something so low-key that it won't really matter one way or the other. Play around with the Associative Post-Hypnotic Suggestion (APHS) described in the last chapter. Make yourself smile at the sound of your lover's voice or sing Elvis in the shower. Use a full session to hypnotise yourself to tidy up your desk or be friendlier to animals or enjoy a particular TV programme. View these early experiments with the trance state as pre-season practice. This approach will reduce the pressure for success, ease your mind and get you in shape for the Big Game.

I'm still not getting the results I want. Is there a short cut?

Let's say you've set well-defined, short-term, low-pressure goals for your self-hypnosis. You've tried the technique for at least two weeks and you're still not getting any results. Or maybe you're doing fine but simply want to save a lot of time working your way down into deep trance. Call a professional. Find a good hypnotherapist.

There are dozens of associations that can put you in contact with a reputable hypnotherapist. At this point in the development of the profession, you're just as likely to find a suitable hypnotherapist in the phone book or through a newspaper or magazine advertisement. However you hear of someone, *call the hypnotherapist first.* Establish your goal: trance depth. Unless you want hypnotherapy, don't let him or her convince you to come in for treatment. (Be prepared; they're bound to suggest it.) Simply say, 'I want to try this on my own first. If I still have trouble later, I'd be prepared to listen to your suggestions. But right now, all I want is a nice deep trance.' If you like the hypnotherapist on the phone, if you get on well, book a session.

Once the hypnotherapist agrees that trance depth – and only trance depth – is the goal, tell him or her that you'd appreciate a few tests to establish your success. Ask the hypnotherapist to give you an APHS that will let you put yourself back into the deep trance at will. (I recommend that you ask the hypnotist to implant an APHS that says anytime you tug your ear lobe and say the word 'sleep', you'll sink into a deep trance. Whatever trigger command you both decide on, make sure it's something you're not likely to do by mistake.) Then sit back, relax and enjoy the ride. Once you've experienced a deep trance and have a 'trap door' to get back, you'll find it much easier to put the trance state to work for you. Remember, even if the APHS is successful, you'll need to do your normal breathing and trance-deepening exercises.

I'm not so sure self-hypnosis is for me. What should I do?

Keep at it! Rome wasn't built in a day; your subconscious wasn't programmed overnight. No matter what does or does not happen with your self-hypnosis, focused relaxation is always therapeutic. At the very least, you will learn how to introduce a measure of peace and calm into your day. So why not give yourself the time you need to get self-hypnosis to work for you? You have from now until the end of your life to get it right. Keep your expectations in line with reality. Self-hypnosis is not *the* answer; it's a technique that can help you *find* an answer.

The only condition for success in self-hypnosis is that you must never give up hope. Many clients who come to the clinic say, 'You're my last hope – I've tried everything!' Everything? Hardly. Most clients have attempted to solve their problem with less than two other types of therapy. Self-hypnosis is a complementary therapy; you're free to try other approaches at the same time. There are easily a dozen different therapies you can sample while practising self-hypnosis. Aromatherapy, gestalt, clinical nutrition, exercise, yoga, T'ai Chi, meditation, prayer, faith-healing, NLP (Neuro-Linguistic Programming), rebirthing, chaksa cleansing, homoeopathy, osteopathy – who knows which key may help unlock the door? Check your local New Age newspaper or bookstore for possibilities. Ask your friends what they've tried. The only therapy I *don't* recommend you try while practising self-hypnosis is traditional psychotherapy. The techniques described in HypnoHealth are based on pure positive thinking. Dredging up past trauma will distract you from focusing on a positive future.

Of course, you should also consider hiring a good hypnotherapist. Don't forget that there are many different types of hypnotherapy – from past-life regression to psychoanalytic to command (the sort you've learned here). Ask the practitioner to describe his particular brand. How does it work? What's the goal? How many sessions do you need? If one type of hypnotherapy doesn't work or appeal, try another.

Above all, never give up. I know there are dark days when it seems that nothing in the world will ever shift your problem. I know there are times when it seems that you're somehow defective and 'bad'. Survive those days! Come through them, put them behind you and soldier on. Try and do it with a song in your heart – even if it's the blues. There is nothing in the world more important than your attitude. It's your first and last line of defence against cruel fate and self-destruction. Tell yourself that whatever ails you, it's not half as bad as losing hope. Tell yourself that 'that which doesn't kill me makes me strong'.

Tell yourself *anything*, but never give up! No matter how trivial or life-threatening your problem, the only failure is to stop trying.

Index

ABOUT THE AUTHOR

Robert Farago was born in Providence, Rhode Island, USA.
After graduating from Tufts University, he worked as a
reporter/editor for Cable News Network in Atlanta, Georgia.
Farago then broke his ankle in a parachute accident, quit his
job, travelled around the world, moved to England, married
Caroline and received hypnotherapy to stop smoking. He then
trained with the London School of Hypnotherapy (UK) and
The National Guild of Hypnotists (US). In 1991, Farago
established a private practice in Flask Walk, Hampstead. For
his own relaxation, Farago practices Wing Chun Kung-Fu,
blasts around the countryside in a TVR Chimaera 4.3 and
discusses politics with his five-month-old daughter Rachel.

**The Farago Clinic offers self-hypnosis tapes, one-to-
one hypnotherapy and group sessions. To contact the
Clinic, telephone 0171 431 1959.**

If you have enjoyed

HypnoHealth

you may also be interested in the following titles
also published by Vermilion

How to Stop Smoking and Stay Stopped for Good (£5.99)

Think Slim (£8.99)

Mind Power (£6.99)

To obtain your copy, simply telephone Murlyn Services on

0279 427203

Your copy will be dispatched to you without delay,
postage and packing free. You may pay by cheque/postal
order/VISA and should allow 28 days for delivery.

**The Longest Journey Starts with a Single Step
Continue Your Journey to Health and Happiness Now!
Order your Farago Clinic Self-Hypnosis Tape**

Quantity	Description	Price	Total
....	Lose Weight Now	@ £9.99	....
....	Confidence!	@ £9.99	....
....	Stop Smoking Now!!	@ £9.99	....
....	Deep Sleep	@ £9.99	....
....	Stress Busters	@ £9.99	....
....	Pain Control	@ £9.99	....
....	Fearless Flying	@ £9.99	....
....	Body Confidence	@ £9.99	....
....	Great Sex	@ £9.99	....
....	Easy Birth	@ £9.99	....
....	*HypnoHealth* [book]	@ £7.99	....

Sub-Total ....

plus postage & packing ....**.60p**

TOTAL ....

Make your cheque payable to:
  The Farago Clinic

Send your cheque or postal order to:
  The Farago Clinic
  PO Box 506
  London SE99 7UY

Please allow 28 days for delivery.